ANTI-RACIST TEACHING

ANTI-RACIST TEACHING

8 STEPS TO BUILD A FRAMEWORK FOR DIVERSITY, EQUITY, AND INCLUSION IN YOUR SCHOOL

SYMONE JAMES ABIOLA

Anti-Racist Teaching
© 2024 by Times 10 Publications
Highland Heights, OH 44143 USA
Website: 10publications.com

All rights reserved. It is illegal to reproduce copies of this work in print or electronic format (including reproductions displayed on a secure intranet or stored in a retrieval system or other electronic storage device from which copies can be made or displayed) without the prior written permission of the publisher, except by a reviewer, who may quote brief passages in a review. For information regarding permission, contact the publisher at editorial@10publications.com. Times 10 Publications books are available at special discounts when purchased in quantity for premiums, promotions, fundraising, and educational use. For inquiries and details, contact us at 10publications.com.

All web links in this book are correct as of the publication date but may have become inactive or otherwise modified since that time. Name brands should not be considered endorsements by the author or Times 10 Publications.

Cover and Interior Design by Steven Plummer
Project Management by Regina Bell
Editing by Tarah Threadgill
Copyediting by Jennifer Jas

Paperback ISBN: 978-1-956512-56-4
eBook ISBN: 978-1-956512-58-8
Hardcover ISBN: 978-1-956512-57-1

Library of Congress Cataloging-in-Publication Data is available for this title.

First Printing: August 2024

To all my former students: You made me grow,
brought me joy, and inspired these words.

TABLE OF CONTENTS

Letter to the Reader 9

INTRODUCTION 11
What Is Anti-Racist Education, and Why Is It Important?

HACK 1: Cultivate Inclusive Classrooms 17
Utilize Inclusive Curricula and Culturally Responsive and Sustaining Pedagogy

HACK 2: Create Sustainable Structures 49
Distribute Leadership for Anti-Racist Efforts

HACK 3: Foster Shared Understandings 69
Plan Meaningful Professional Learning Opportunities

HACK 4: Provide Ongoing Support 91
Offer Teachers Personalized and Whole-School Support

HACK 5: Intentionally Support BIPOC Educators 111
Recruit and Retain with Purpose

HACK 6: Get Students Engaged 137
Create Opportunities for Students to Be Actively Involved

HACK 7: Invite Family Participation 157
Welcome Families into the School Community

HACK 8: Plan for Longevity 179
Create a Framework so These Efforts Will Last

CONCLUSION 199
Keep Moving Forward

About the Author 203
Acknowledgments 205
Sneak Peek: *Hacking Culturally Inclusive Teaching* 207
More from Times 10 Publications 219

LETTER TO THE READER

DEAR READER,

I'M A *BIG* crier. Movies, happy moments, goodbyes, it doesn't matter. So, when I first received news that I would have the honor of writing a book for Times 10 Publications, I (embarrassingly) bawled in front of my student teacher and a class full of fifth graders. I have been fortunate to experience plenty of amazing learning opportunities throughout my years as a student at the University of Connecticut (go Huskies!); a teacher; and a diversity, equity, and inclusion practitioner. I hope that through this book, I can share what I've learned in a practical way that supports you and other educators in implementing lasting changes in your schools. In reality, we cannot literally hack anti-racist teaching and learning; however, we can take realistic and achievable steps, starting today and over time, to initiate and sustain endeavors rooted in anti-racism.

When I think about the educators I admire most, I've always felt that one of their greatest strengths is their willingness to share and collaborate. This belief is why, over my years as a teacher, I said yes to almost every invitation to collaborate with other educators in diversity, equity, and inclusion work. By working together to support our students, we learn from and support each other in providing the best school experience. As a Black, first-generation American and first-generation college graduate, this topic is personal. As I grew up, education was highly valued in my home. I was taught that success in education meant more opportunities. However, this belief didn't protect my sister or me from experiencing racism from teachers or peers. These situations undoubtedly played a role in my identity development, academic performance, and overall school engagement. They are common for many Black, Indigenous, and other students of color today, and it comes with severe consequences for many.

As you read this book, I hope you realize that it doesn't have to be that way. Countless resources exist to create school environments that uplift students and provide the support they need to thrive. *Anti-Racist Teaching* serves as a resource with specific strategies to help you and your school do just that. With a growth mindset and collaboration, you can reimagine the way school has always been "done" and refine practices and policies to truly provide an equitable education for all students.

– Symone James Abiola

INTRODUCTION

WHAT IS ANTI-RACIST EDUCATION, AND WHY IS IT IMPORTANT?

IN 1947, THE *Mendez v. Westminster* case successfully challenged segregation in education. It set a precedent for the more widely known case, *Brown v. Board of Education,* which deemed racial segregation in schools unconstitutional. However, many years later, students are still experiencing the legacy of longstanding racist systems, policies, and beliefs. Educators have a professional responsibility to do what is best for *all* students, including educating them in an environment that ensures they have the best chance to achieve success. To do this for all students, we must:

- **Look inward:** Understand the role of our own identities within these systems, consider how we uphold these policies, and question the beliefs we possess (and be open to growing)

- **Look outward:** Become aware of racist systems, policies, and beliefs in the past and present that continue to negatively impact students
- **Be proactive:** Take action to change the systems, policies, and beliefs that harm students

We must also recognize the influence of intersectionality, a term coined by Kimberlé Crenshaw in an academic paper in 1989. In *We Want to Do More Than Survive*, Dr. Bettina Love describes the meaning of this term as a "necessary analytic tool to explain the complexities and the realities of discrimination and of power or the lack thereof, and how they intersect with identities." In other words, our culture, language, race, gender, sexuality, ability, religion, and spirituality all intertwine to affect our lives with varying levels of discrimination, power, and privilege. It is crucial that we recognize the experiences of Black, Indigenous, and other students of color; those who are LGBTQ+; those who possess exceptionalities; and students who share other historically marginalized identities. The steps and changes I recommend throughout this book will help your school or district to put systems in place that create a framework for diversity, equity, and inclusion (DEI), which, when done well, helps to create a school environment that acknowledges and values the many identities our students possess. Anti-racism is a critical part of DEI work that proactively addresses racism and bias. When we intentionally affirm, value, respect, nurture, and care for the whole student, we can approach education through an anti-racist lens.

While this book focuses on anti-racism, many other aspects of DEI work must be pursued. We can strive to create schools that acknowledge and address all forms of bias, prejudice, and discrimination and provide the school community members with support to enhance their critical consciousness, understanding of identity, and agency to advocate for themselves and others.

Anti-racist work not only takes time, but it is also ongoing and unending as we make improvements and respond with flexibility to current needs and challenges. Anti-racist and DEI efforts will not be without opposition. Folks will always push back, disagree, and avoid seeing the purpose in changing the situation. As educators, we must be honest in asking ourselves and others, "Are we doing what's best for all students?"

Anti-racist education requires us to develop the courage to have tough conversations and the motivation to do what is best for students, even in the face of discomfort and controversy. For some, efforts toward a more racially equitable school will be welcome, while for others, it might bring out the worst within the school community. However, we must determine our core values as educators and put students first.

You may question whether your school needs to educate students through an anti-racist lens if it is predominantly white. The answer is emphatically *"yes."* Anti-racist education prepares *all* students for the vastly diverse world around them, provides a richer education by teaching truth and critical thinking, and particularly supports students in recognizing their own racial biases and beliefs they may have already developed. This type of education does *not* mean making students feel bad about their race, and it *does* mean fostering an awareness of identity and an understanding of how they can take action to create a more socially just society.

Anti-racist education requires us to find areas for growth within our school and within ourselves to make necessary changes that will ultimately improve outcomes for students. These positive outcomes include academic achievement, social and emotional growth, authentic connections between students and educators, and a greater sense of empathy for one another. Importantly, when we create environments that are inclusive and affirming, and when we educate students to develop a great critical consciousness, we support their growth as individuals with agency and the ability to advocate for others. With a growth mindset and commitment to centering students and supporting educators, we can create environments where all students can thrive.

If you are skimming through the Introduction (like I sometimes do), please read this:

Whether you are a teacher, DEI practitioner, building or district leader, or part of the education workforce in another role, the eight Hacks shared in this book will help you make a positive, lasting difference in your school community and provide support to educators. I even suggest reading this book as a team because, ultimately, achieving the goals of anti-racist education takes a collaborative effort. Changes to create a school environment that authentically values anti-racism cannot be siloed, and everyone, especially school leaders, needs to support efforts for the changes to be effective.

Each chapter follows the Hack Learning Series template, with sections that explain The Problem, The Hack, What You Can Do Tomorrow, A Blueprint for Full Implementation, Overcoming Pushback, and The Hack in Action. Each Hack offers practical solutions for making anti-racist education the bedrock of your classroom and your school.

You'll notice that I end this book with Hack 8, a chapter on recommendations for longevity. One could argue that this content should go first. However, the breadth and depth of my recommendations in Hack 8 require a long-term commitment and a team of people to inform and staunchly support the progress of those recommendations—a team that you can create by following the guidance in Hack 2. In Hack 8, I also strongly recommend recruiting someone whose sole job is to lead diversity, equity, and inclusion efforts. Having a role dedicated to the evolution and growth of programs, policies, and practices is a highly effective step. It also signals your institution's commitment to progress.

Depending on your school's growth in these areas, adopt the contents of this book as a whole or utilize the parts you need the most. There are no rules or limits. Every school is different; you may be reading this from a large public school district perspective or from a small private school setting. Start where you can, skip around chapters, and go back when necessary. Progress is not always linear, and I invite you to connect with me anytime to discuss the ideas in this book and how they could work in your school. Additionally, you can find resources mentioned throughout the book on symonejamesabiola.com.

HACK 1

CULTIVATE INCLUSIVE CLASSROOMS
UTILIZE INCLUSIVE CURRICULA AND CULTURALLY RESPONSIVE AND SUSTAINING PEDAGOGY

If we are truly a great nation, the truth cannot destroy us.
— Nikole Hannah-Jones, investigative reporter

THE PROBLEM: CURRICULA AND CLASSROOM EXPERIENCES CENTER WHITENESS

To create more inclusive classrooms and practice antiracist teaching, we must disrupt the status quo of centering whiteness. In her book *Me and White Supremacy,* author, speaker, and teacher Layla Saad explains that "White centering is the centering of white people, white values, white norms, and white feelings over everything and everyone else." So often, curricula used in classrooms and schools centers whiteness, with the special occasion exception of resources used to celebrate holidays and heritage months. This type of learning environment sends the message to BIPOC students (Black, Indigenous, and other people of color) that who they are is not as valued as their white peers. For white students, it sends the opposite message: their experiences, cultural histories, values, and the people who look like them are "the norm" and valued more than all others.

White centering is due to the history of racism and white supremacy. Black, Indigenous, and other people of color in the United States have historically been seen and treated as the "other" in schools and society at large. What and how we teach continue to reflect this belief, consciously and unconsciously, unless we actively change our pedagogy. In schools where most of the teacher population is white, it may not be a surprise that many educators are teaching in ways and using materials that connect to how they likely participated in K–12 education as students. Some teachers work in environments where expectations of curricula are dictated to them, and they are not afforded much choice about how to teach Tier 1 lessons, including the materials they can use. Other teachers may not know how to facilitate critical conversations or the best ways to insert supplemental materials. No matter the reason, these teaching decisions can have a lasting negative impact on students.

THE HACK: CULTIVATE INCLUSIVE CLASSROOMS

We can intentionally build inclusive classrooms by employing Culturally Responsive and Sustaining Pedagogy (CRSP), which builds on the framework of Culturally Relevant Teaching coined by education theorist Gloria Ladson-Billings. To lay the groundwork for this process, we must first understand the meaning of culturally responsive teaching (CRT). Here's a definition from Zaretta Hammond, author of *Culturally Responsive Teaching and the Brain*. She wrote that CRT is "an educator's ability to recognize students' cultural displays of learning and meaning-making and respond positively and constructively with teaching moves that use cultural knowledge as a scaffold to connect what the students know to new concepts and content in order to promote effective information processing. All the while, the educator understands the importance of being in relationship and having a social-emotional connection to the student to create a safe space for learning." Culturally Sustaining Pedagogy (CSP), a term offered by Django Paris, "seeks to perpetuate and foster—to sustain—linguistic, literate, and cultural pluralism as part of schooling for positive social transformation" to maintain the multilingualism and multiculturalism of communities while also giving access to the dominant culture."

> **WE FAIL IN OUR DUTY TO EDUCATE WHEN WE AVOID CHALLENGING CONVERSATIONS, WE SEE STUDENTS THROUGH A DEFICIT LENS, AND OUR ACTIONS (OR LACK OF ACTIONS) REVEAL THAT WE VALUE SOME IDENTITIES OVER OTHERS.**

With these definitions in mind, CRSP enables educators to meet students where they are to better serve their needs, expands students' worldviews, encourages deeper discourse, provides more meaningful materials, and creates a more affirming environment that nurtures students' identity development and sense of belonging. All this lends itself toward high-quality academic preparation and deeper critical consciousness for all students. By using these pathways to cultivate an inclusive classroom, we can create environments where deepening students' sense of empathy and strengthening their sense of self are woven into the fabric of teaching and learning, not outcomes that we just hope will happen.

No matter your school environment, it benefits students and society to educate in ways that build connections among students and develop their understanding of the world. We fail in our duty to educate when we avoid challenging conversations, we see students through a deficit lens, and our actions (or lack of actions) reveal that we value some identities over others. This Hack will help you thoughtfully plan, use inclusive curricula, and develop the pedagogical capacity of educators. These maneuvers will create school and classroom environments that value and affirm diverse identities while supporting the academic achievement of all students.

While I do share some schoolwide suggestions, many of the actions offer practical steps educators can take in the classroom. Please keep in mind that this chapter provides an overview and is not meant to be an all-inclusive guide to Culturally Responsive and Sustaining Pedagogy; you can find many great books that go deep on this subject. If you are in a role outside of the classroom, such as an administrator, coach, or DEI practitioner, consider how you can support teachers to make these suggestions feasible and make CRSP *the* mindset and foundation of teaching and learning.

WHAT YOU CAN DO TOMORROW

Before we jump into long-term recommendations, let's first figure out what we know. Here, I suggest you collect some data on yourself, and later, we'll collect data about students. As you consider these reflection questions, know that they are meant to help you grow, not offer a finite conclusion of your practice as an educator. As you answer, go beyond what you *intend* to do and contemplate actual evidence to support your answers.

- **Personally reflect on your beliefs and practices.** It might feel like a personal suggestion, and it's meant to; it's all about you. As educators, when the job becomes challenging, we might attempt to compartmentalize and keep work at work and our personal lives personal. I know I have. But let's be real: while this can be a healthy practice in some situations, we still bring our whole selves to work just as students do. If we want to be antiracist educators, we must get personal and look inward—not only at what we do in the classroom but at the beliefs and practices we bring with us to our jobs. We must consider how they influence the way we teach and our relationships with students, staff, and families. Get a piece of paper and jot down your thoughts about the following questions. They will serve as a start to deeper reflection that will guide your next steps.

    ▸ How have you pursued personal growth in the last five years? Think broadly, not only as an educator but also as a human. Have you intentionally sought to uncover and address your own biases?

    ▸ What personal and educational beliefs or core values do you hold dearly, and what actions have you taken in your classroom or school because of them? How do they show up in the activities and with the people you engage with outside of school?

- What is your reaction when faced with uncomfortable or hard conversations?
- What constitutes uncomfortable or hard topics for you to discuss?
- If you had to describe your identities, how would you do so? Which identities do you think most about?

- **Look around your room and school.** As a teacher, one of my favorite tasks was to decorate the classroom, but I know not everyone shares this joy. I felt gratification in envisioning an environment my students and I would enjoy and then making that vision come to life. Over time, I got better at considering the purpose of the items in our room. Did I choose it because it looked nice, or did it add value to our space? Whether you are a minimalist teacher, a maximalist, or someone who does not have a permanent room, the skill of discerning the message and meaning that students gather from their environment is a significant one. Whether or not it is intentional, our educational spaces tell students about ourselves. They can also provide chances for students to see themselves and people and ideas that are new to them. Consider these questions about your classroom, office, or school spaces.
    - Do decorations portraying people offer a diverse representation? A diverse representation goes beyond race and includes ethnicity, cultural identifiers, socioeconomic

status, age, religious beliefs, nationality, neurodiversity, ability, sex, sexual orientation, and gender.

- Do decorations or other items in the space add value to your instruction, support building community, align with your behavior management practices, or set the vibe (such as calming, uplifting) you desire for your space?
- How many of the items in your space were created by or contributed by students, such as student work, art, or letters?
- What items in your space represent you as a person, not only as an educator? These could include pictures of family and friends, moments of special events, or hobbies you enjoy.

• **Build community in the classroom.** Community is crucial. When we take the time to build community within our classrooms, we are investing in our students' ability to empathize with each other, develop communication skills, and increase their sense of safety and resiliency. During my first couple years of teaching fifth grade, I had the honor of working with a team that taught me so much. One of the teachers was committed to holding restorative circles during our social-emotional learning time. Whenever an incident occurred, her class knew how to gather and work through the issue. It wasn't

Anti-Racist Teaching

just a coincidence; it was because this teacher had spent intentional time building community and fostering relationships that students could work through conflicts in a healthy way that deepened their empathy and understanding of each other. I was a new teacher, and this method of conflict resolution was an invaluable example of the power of building and strengthening community and the strategies I could use when classroom issues arose. Consider these questions for reflection.

- What actions do you take to intentionally build community *throughout* the year?
- How does your class handle conflict, and what do you purposefully teach students about handling conflict?
- In what ways have you seen students hold themselves and others accountable?
- What do students do when they need help with a situation?
- How do you share the "emotional load" of working through problems with your class?
- What do students do if they disagree with you, and how do you react?

A BLUEPRINT FOR FULL IMPLEMENTATION

Step 1: Start with yourself.

In the previous section, you engaged in personal reflection, gaining insights about how our identities and experiences shape our beliefs, values, and cultural perceptions. These, in turn, impact our pedagogy and relationships with students, especially those from historically marginalized populations. In *Culturally Responsive Teaching and the Brain*, Zaretta Hammond wrote that educators must develop their sociopolitical lens to understand the role of our identities within society and the unearned privilege or disadvantage attached to these identities based on race, class, gender, and other identifiers. Collectively, we all benefit when we understand how racism and other forms of prejudice and discrimination have shaped the larger political context in which we live and educate. If you have yet to take time to reflect on your identities within these contexts, here are a few suggestions to begin understanding your own positionality.

> **WE ALL BENEFIT WHEN WE UNDERSTAND HOW RACISM AND OTHER FORMS OF PREJUDICE AND DISCRIMINATION HAVE SHAPED THE LARGER POLITICAL CONTEXT IN WHICH WE LIVE AND EDUCATE.**

You can find these two activities online, and they will help to guide you in determining your identities. First, search for a Social and Personal Identity Wheel. One option is the identity wheel adapted from "Voices of Discovery," Intergroup Relations Center, Arizona State University; however, many other options are also appropriate. Next, see where the identities you possess fall on the Wheel of Power and Privilege originally created by the Canadian Council for Refugees. Notable adapted versions of this wheel have been created by Sylvia Duckworth and Tessa Watkins, but again, many options are available.

When you complete this activity, reflect on whether you are closer to the center for some identities and to the outer margins for others.

Seek resources to learn how privilege serves certain identities while others are met with barriers, and what those barriers may be. What about your students? Having a critical consciousness of positionality and privilege will help you recognize and critique the effect of privilege within our society and understand how systems inequitably and unjustly serve certain populations. Consider how this is evident within schools and even between school districts. An awareness of privilege prompts us to act when we recognize our own harmful practices and roles within problematic systems. You can find self-assessment resources in the book *Using Equity Audits in the Classroom to Reach and Teach All Students* by Kathryn McKenzie and Linda Skrla.

Step 2: Get to know your students and build relationships.

Knowing your students is critical. How else can we begin to understand their needs and what makes them who they are? Getting to know students beyond data on their behavior, attendance, or academic history takes intentional, continuous efforts throughout the year. While these elements are necessary, we can absolutely go deeper. What triggers them? How do they know they are valued, appreciated, or cared for? How will you know they trust you? What makes them "light up" in the classroom? What are their talents? Do they have consistent food, shelter, and clean clothing? Do they feel safe? These are a few questions to consider, but when you think about how well you know your students, be comprehensive and don't make assumptions about their basic needs. When students' basic needs are not being met, they undergo negative consequences in a host of ways, and it would be illogical for us to expect them to come to school with the capacity to focus on the subject we are teaching. Here are strategies to learn about your students, make connections, and build relationships.

- Hold consistent check-ins: These can be brief, open-ended conversations to check in with students. They might happen during transitions, arrival or dismissal, or any other convenient time. Check-ins can be systematic and planned for individuals or the whole class. They are meaningful for all students over the course of the school week and may be particularly significant for students who are more introverted.

- Give individualized greetings every day: Make it a habit to greet every student by the name they have asked to be called as they enter our classrooms as a sign of acknowledgment and to set a positive tone for the day. At the beginning of each year, I shared why this was valuable to me and why I had the expectation of them offering a greeting in return. Moving forward, whenever I didn't receive a greeting back, I learned that it was usually a signal that something was "off," and I needed to check in with that student before the day began.

- Provide one-on-one and small-group conversations: These are longer than check-ins and great ways to learn more about students. Keep the group small with two or three students. It could take the form of a "lunch bunch" (when students and their teacher have lunch together), a small group at the end of instruction, or non-academic student conferences.

- Deploy student interest surveys or get-to-know-you inventories: Tons of free examples are available online. Interest surveys and get-to-know-you inventories are great tools to learn more about your students' interests, talents, motivations, and lives outside of school. They also provide information for you to follow up on as you have conversations.

- Schedule morning meetings, advisory meetings, or other classroom community gatherings: Take time to build community by coming together as a class for non-academic reasons. Whether you call this advisory time, homeroom, or morning meetings, create time and space to allow students to share about themselves and learn about one another. Plan activities and conversations with the intention of connecting. You might also use this time to engage in social-emotional learning.

- Offer methods for student feedback: While more assertive students may share their thoughts, opinions, and stories of encounters throughout the school year, creating a system to collect feedback from everyone provides valuable insights. One example is the "Teacher Report Card" that I implemented. Three times a year, at the same time as student report cards, students would complete a paper or digital copy of a Teacher Report Card about me. These offered feedback that helped me make intentional changes in our classroom environment and learn about the students. These report cards asked students to rate or answer questions such as:
  - My teacher treats all students fairly.
  - My teacher recognizes when I work hard.
  - Is there anything you would suggest we change about our classroom?

Step 3: Create a welcoming and affirming environment.

Getting to know students also helps tailor the environment to who they are and their needs. Simultaneously, we must create a welcoming and affirming environment for students to feel secure. Not only is this best for their social-emotional wellness, but it also helps students feel safe in their learning and willing to take risks. I define the "environment" as both the physical space that students are in and the climate and culture within those spaces.

- Physical environment: What do students see? As stated earlier, the items we include in educational spaces matter. My suggested features of classroom and school décor include:
    ▸ Imagery that offers a diverse representation of people and ideas, particularly positive representations of historically marginalized identities
    ▸ Visuals that offer encouraging images and messages
    ▸ Student work (without grades)
    ▸ Useful tools, such as anchor charts, visual aids for lessons, or behavioral tools (i.e., Zones of Regulation posters, calming strategies, and school expectations)

- Culture and climate: School culture encompasses the values, practices, and beliefs of members of the school community. School climate is what we feel because of the culture. Schools can strive to foster a culture of care. Leaning on the teachings of Geneva Gay and Zaretta Hammond, a culture of care is characterized by affirmation, mutual respect, and validation. From our greetings when students enter school to the way we address and discuss challenging behaviors, all of our actions speak to the culture and, in turn, define the actualized experiences of students. The following list is in no way complete, but here are ten principles that are necessary to create an environment where students feel cared for, respected, and affirmed:

- Respond to behaviors in a way that maintains dignity and mutual respect for yourself and your students. If you ever fail to do so, apologize.
- Allow and invite students to share their feedback about classroom discussions and situations. Then, take their feedback and use it to inform decisions and make changes.
- Strive to develop relationships and do what we can to provide support. There are no inherently bad kids; however, students can make poor decisions and display challenging behavior. Often, we can't alleviate the root cause of behavioral challenges, but we can seek to understand, have empathy, support their character development, and respond to behaviors in an informed way.
- Hold all students to high expectations and regularly offer positive affirmations. What we say and hear about ourselves matters.
- Offer fresh starts while still holding students accountable. Be someone who offers grace when a student is having a bad day or year.
- Follow up, check in, and vocally let students know you are there for support if needed, especially if they've shared emotional information or a feeling or opinion that you disagree with. It benefits everyone to listen with understanding.
- Listen when a student tells you they feel a situation isn't fair. They might not have the language yet to describe bias, discrimination, or racism, but they are excellent at discerning fairness.

- Be vulnerable with your students. Of course, we must be mindful of what we share, but our vulnerability signals to students that they can be vulnerable as well, and it also helps us to develop deeper, authentic relationships. Additionally, it's okay not to know things. As the adult in the room, we might feel like we need to have all the answers, but that's impossible. It's okay to admit what we don't know and seek more information.

- Respect boundaries and personal space. I want to note that this includes students' hair. Hair is a part of any individual's personal space and is not to be touched without asking. It is a microaggression and can come with legal ramifications in some states. Even if one asks for permission, it's uncomfortable to want to say no and feel as though you're offending the other person. If you see it happen between students, address it promptly. For Black girls and women in particular, the complex histories around our hair make this a loaded action.

Step 4: Review and update your curriculum.

What and how we teach is critical, but often, it can be a hard element to change due to expectations set by your school, district, or state. However, if we believe in doing what is best for students, we must interrogate whether the curricula used in classrooms offer a high-quality, meaningful, and engaging education for all students. We can do this by utilizing inclusive curricula. In "Exploring the Growth of Inclusive Curriculum: A Systematic Review of Scholar and Practitioner Perspectives," Amelie Smucker describes an inclusive curriculum as one that "(a) addresses discrimination, (b) meets the needs of all students, and (c) encompasses content, pedagogy, and assessment methods. Additionally, an inclusive curriculum is welcoming, accessible, challenging, flexible, intentional, and authentic." Ideally, materials and resources will incorporate a truly diverse representation of identities, experiences, and perspectives, while methods of teaching, learning, and assessment offer students various pathways to exhibit their learning.

- Review the curriculum. The process might look different depending on your personal role and school setting. Some teachers must create their curriculum for the year only guided by state standards, thus, individual teachers are all teaching different concepts via different methods; other schools might use scripted lessons, with everyone teaching in the same way. No matter the case, review the content and material with a critical lens. Here are a few guiding questions:
    - ▶ Whose perspectives are represented? Specifically, are historically marginalized populations represented? If so, are there positive representations?
    - ▶ Think of *each* student you work with and the multitude of identities they possess; where and how do students see themselves represented?
    - ▶ How does it maintain high academic expectations with a variety of entry points for all students to understand and demonstrate learning?
    - ▶ What are the methods for formative and summative assessment? Do they consider students with exceptionalities, students who are English Language Learners, and cultural nuances?
    - ▶ Are there opportunities to discuss issues of inequality and inequity, help students develop

a critical consciousness, and explore global perspectives?

  ▶ What methods are used to allow students to have voice and choice in their learning?

- Determine what needs to be removed, added, and revised based on these questions, as well as considerations for your school, district, and state guidelines. Sometimes, we already have a great starting point that we can improve upon, and other times, we need to reimagine the entire foundation.

- Start making changes with input. It's always a best practice to get perspectives and feedback from a diverse group of individuals when we make changes that will have a significant impact on students and the instructional core. If you have a diversity, equity, and inclusion team (or a related team), they can be a source of input and guidance.

- Be purposeful about supplemental materials. Supplemental books and other resources offer a way to add whatever you feel your core curriculum is missing. I often used small-group instruction and special projects to insert materials that incorporated more culturally relevant and sustaining activities and content, as well as content that I felt would expand students' global perspectives and deepen critical consciousness.

This is a pared-down guide to making curricular changes, a process that can take years. Be mindful that this undertaking can look different depending on your school structure, leadership, support, and resources. We must do what we can with what we have to improve students' experiences.

Step 5: Set the stage for difficult conversations.

A hallmark of CRSP that is critical to anti-racism is the development of a safe and brave environment where students are willing to take risks in their learning, engage in conversations that deepen their critical consciousness, develop their sense of empathy for diverse perspectives and cultures, and challenge racist, biased, discriminatory, and bigoted ideas. However, these types of spaces don't just happen by accident. Here are three suggestions to set the stage so students feel comfortable engaging in these discussions and environments.

- Collectively determine shared values through community agreements and norms. It's always a good practice to create classroom contracts or agreements together at the beginning of the year, and you can also develop a set of norms specifically for discussions. Not only does this help you understand the values that students are coming in with, but you can also create a foundation for how your classroom community holds each other accountable and maintains an atmosphere of shared responsibility and mutual respect.

- Address incidents of microaggressions, racism, discrimination, and bigotry. Addressing them is a key action to build trust and create safe environments for students. If you witness an exchange, an incident is brought to your attention, or a student trusts you enough to share, be sure to listen to understand and do not invalidate their experience. It's only the start of the conversation and may necessitate continued processing with other supportive adults, such as a school counselor, as well as the next steps for accountability and further learning for others involved.

- Create spaces that are safe for students to discuss challenging topics, including current events. It's necessary for students to feel seen and heard and that we create opportunities for them to engage in discussions about difficult subjects and welcome conversations that come up organically. Whether conversations take place one on one, in a small group, via the whole class, or with the whole school, we must be prepared to support students in navigating their questions and emotions after experiencing personal or collective events. I recommend learning about different structures and suggestions for facilitating challenging conversations, as the strategies and skills needed will look different depending on the age of students.

Step 6: Check your library.

Cultivating a diverse classroom and school library is crucial. It's not a new idea. In 1988, Emily Style introduced the metaphor "windows and mirrors" to the education space. The metaphor, shared in her essay "Curriculum As Window and Mirror," helped educators understand why it is important for students to learn about different people, experiences, and perspectives (windows) and also to see themselves reflected in the curriculum (mirrors). In 1990, Dr. Rudine Sims Bishop expanded the idea of "windows and mirrors" in her piece "Mirrors, Windows, and Sliding Glass Doors" and made the connection to multicultural literature. She explains that windows are also sliding glass doors, and "readers only have to walk through in imagination to become a part of whatever world has been created by the author."

Dr. Sims Bishop's metaphor of "sliding glass doors" put a spotlight on the importance of students going beyond "looking into" experiences different from their own and also becoming immersed, which leads to the development of deeper empathy, understanding, and reflection. While it is common for BIPOC students to be exposed to the points of view of white people, it is absolutely essential for white students to be immersed in multicultural perspectives that are different from their own and for all students to engage in knowledge that invites them to learn about and reflect on a variety of worldviews. If you are unsure of the diversity of your library, here are guiding questions derived from "5 Ways to Audit Your Classroom Library for Inclusion" by Hoa P. Nguyen:

- How many books feature BIPOC people as the main character, not the sidekick?
- How many books feature people who are LGBTQ+, neurodivergent, have different physical abilities, or have various family structures?
- How do books promote or dispel stereotypes?
- How are various languages and cultural heritages represented and honored?

Step 7: Strengthen your personal pedagogy.

So often, I hear educators say, "Kids today are different!" in reference to behaviors that can be challenging, such as the increased reliance on technology and perceived dependence in navigating social issues. On the other hand, positive traits include kids thriving with collaboration, wanting social-emotional development, and courageously engaging in conversations about what some adults consider to be difficult topics, such as race, gender, and sexuality. I cannot say that the children of the past did or did not do these things, but access to technology has absolutely changed the ways in which students engage and learn, as well as the information they are aware of before an adult is willing to discuss it with them. The current environment leads me to ask, "How are we keeping up?" Being lifelong learners and pursuing professional learning are keys to addressing the evolving needs of students.

Throughout this chapter, I've asked questions for you to reflect on. One was, "How have you pursued personal growth in the last five years?" As educators, we must seek out opportunities to grow. While reading this Hack, or even this book, you may be inspired to pursue certain recommendations that highlight areas of professional and personal development. While in-person workshops and conferences are great for growth, they aren't always options due to time and resources. Other avenues to further your knowledge and skills in these areas of teaching and learning include books, webinars, roundtable talks, peer walkthroughs, in-school learning tours, podcasts, articles, peer-reviewed papers, professional learning communities, and collaboration with peers in and outside of your school. I know it is difficult to make professional learning a priority outside of work, but the more informed we are and the more we develop our skills, the greater capacity we'll have to do our jobs and feel confident in the results of our practices. You will benefit by adding more tools to your toolbox for whatever role you are in. I suggest choosing a personal aspiration for each school year and engaging in learning about it through any of the avenues listed earlier. Then, set a realistic goal for yourself each month to learn through a selected avenue. Keep track of any resources you collect and suggestions that you find meaningful. As we gain knowledge, it's essential to explore how we can apply it to our work. Here are ideas for topics to delve into:

- Culturally responsive, relevant, sustaining practices
- Restorative practices and relationship-building strategies
- Understanding and responding to racial trauma
- Addressing incidents of racism, discrimination, bias, and bigotry

Anti-Racist Teaching

- Identity development
- Intersectionality, positionality, and privilege
- How to create safe spaces and facilitate dialogue for students
- Effective instructional strategies (generally and by content area)
- Differentiation and scaffolding
- Instructional practices for student-centered learning
- Serving students with exceptionalities
- Building community in the school and classroom
- Equitable grading practices

OVERCOMING PUSHBACK

Culturally Responsive and Sustaining Pedagogy requires us to first look inward at what we are bringing into the classroom and then develop our capacity to meet the needs of all students. For some educators, this may present challenges. Here are a few possible pushbacks and how to address them.

Teachers are required to stick to the curriculum and state standards, and they don't have time to add extra activities. It is a common misconception that CRSP means adding materials about BIPOC figures or celebrating holidays. While these can be included, the ideas are so much bigger. Hopefully, this Hack has already provided a more detailed picture of what CRSP involves: curriculum, instruction, relationships, climate, and culture—so much more than heroes and holidays. Even if teachers are required to stick to teaching the materials that have been given to them, or if they are prohibited from using certain texts due to state or district policies, they can engage students in deeper, more meaningful thinking and conversation by adjusting how they teach and the questions and discussions in which they engage students. Additionally, there is always more than one way to meet a specific standard. Teaching in culturally responsive ways means that we think about how our learning activities meet certain standards and objectives and are responsive to students' identities, broadening their worldview and challenging them to question systems of inequity.

Additionally, if you are a school leader, keep in mind that supporting educators in delivering more flexible, meaningful, and accessible learning can be a mode of retention for staff and a strategy for increased student engagement and success. When teachers are stripped of the autonomy to adjust their lessons and pacing to the needs of students, it removes much of the joy and creativity that make teaching magical. Rather than teaching to the needs of students in front of you, you begin teaching to test content and deadlines. By supporting the use of an inclusive curriculum and encouraging educators to make responsive pedagogical decisions, teachers can better meet the needs of individual students and make learning meaningful.

A student's race does not matter when everyone is being taught the same content. Culturally Responsive and Sustaining Pedagogy is not just about race. It's about the way each student's brain makes sense of the world around them (again, as shared by Zaretta Hammond). It's about creating an environment where each student has chances to make meaningful connections to their learning and have a strong sense of belonging within their school. You are not expected to deeply understand every student's culture, but as we increase our sociopolitical awareness and develop connections with students, we also get to know who they are and their frames of reference, which, in turn, allows us to provide more personalized learning and help them feel safer in taking risks in their learning.

I will continue to come back to this: our goal as educators is to do what is best for all students, and that means striving toward providing the type of education I described in this Hack. Regardless of whether all students receive the same content, they are making sense of it in different ways. Each of their experiences in your classroom will be different. Each of their experiences with different teachers will be different. We must strive to ensure Black, Indigenous, and other students of color also have adults they can trust and with whom they feel a meaningful connection to their learning.

Our school's professional development has not been high quality, and out-of-school or out-of-district events are expensive. I cannot count how many times I've heard this feedback. I've heard staff lament that the professional development was not relevant or engaging or that it could have been an email. These types of comments are why I included a Hack dedicated to planning for professional learning opportunities. Professional learning is best when it's based on students' needs and what staff requires to meet those needs. It should be engaging and meaningful. Whoever is planning and preparing to provide professional learning must have some knowledge about how adults learn and how the materials can be applied to attendees' roles.

Part of this pushback is that high-quality professional development can be expensive, and it's especially true when looking at professional learning offered by individuals with deep expertise. If you have the resources to send staff to this type of training, please do it. But we know it's not always possible. My first suggestion is that if you are developing the professional capacity of staff to support students while also cultivating leadership, you may have folks who can work together to plan professional learning, which helps to keep costs lower than hiring an outside consultant (although you also need to pay these folks for their time). Additionally, some of the best professional learning you can find is not only offered through conferences and expensive workshops but also by tapping into other educators' knowledge online. Social media is a great place to learn from communities of educators, as well as to access free and low-cost webinars, books, and digital courses.

THE HACK IN ACTION

Tracey Lafayette is an elementary teacher in Connecticut. She attended the Neag School of Education at the University of Connecticut and earned a dual degree in elementary education and English, and minored in Diversity Studies in American Culture. Later in her career, she obtained her administrative certification from the University of Connecticut Administrator Preparation Program. Tracey has been committed to developing her sociopolitical understanding, creating spaces for fellow BIPOC educators to find support, and helping her students understand their identities and evolve in their critical consciousness.

In 2012, *The Daily Campus*, UConn's independent, student-run newspaper, reported the Neag School of Education as having the "lowest percentage of minority students." To some students, this may have been just another fact. To Tracey, who was a student at the time, it was a call to action. Upon learning about the low enrollment and graduation rates of students of color in the Neag School of Education, Tracey and a peer developed the idea for a student group that would support BIPOC students applying to and attending the Neag School of Education. In 2014, Leadership in Diversity, known as L.I.D., became an officially registered student organization. It's one of many initiatives that demonstrated Tracey's drive to take real action when faced with a situation born from inequity.

Tracey's drive continues to inform her actions as an elementary teacher as she enacts change through her work with students. Her kindergarten through fifth grade school serves BIPOC students predominantly, with most students eligible for free or reduced lunch. With every new class, Tracey ingrains the values of diversity and empowerment through her everyday practices, pedagogy, and projects.

Starting at the beginning of the school year, Tracey uses get-to-know-you activities strategically. Not only does she plan activities for students to share about themselves, but she also begins to build up the vocabulary they need to discuss social issues. One example of this is sharing a Word of the Day. Each day, she shares a word like equity, activism, or empowerment and plans activities throughout the day that motivate students to learn about and use this vocabulary. Intentional planning sets up students for success throughout the year. For many of her students, this is the first time they talk about related topics or use this vocabulary in an academic space. By building up their background knowledge and vocabulary, students are not only more prepared to have deeper conversations later on, but they are also having conversations that are meaningful and expanding their understanding of topics relevant to their lives.

Among the many ways that Tracey engages her students in critical conversations about the world around them, her favorite is an activism project she has done yearly since her second year as a teacher, no matter what grade she is teaching. During the opinion-writing unit, students write an opinion piece about a topic of their choice. The topic might come from ideas they heard outside of school or topics they learned about in class. However, she does not simply tell them to pick a topic and get started. Like the way Tracey front-loads vocabulary that students will need as they discuss social issues, she also offers a robust classroom library and utilizes reading throughout the year to teach about social issues such as racism, gender discrimination, diversity, homelessness, and environmentalism. For students, this activism project begins when they sit together and brainstorm ideas. During this time, she does not offer any sort of feedback aside from asking for

Cultivate Inclusive Classrooms

clarification. They share ideas that they are already thinking about and come up with organically. See Image 1 for an example.

Image 1: Students brainstorm causes to fight for or against.

Next, the students dive into research and writing about their topics. Throughout this opinion-writing project, students learn the writing skills they need to create strong opinion pieces as well as other key academic skills such as grammar, spelling, and punctuation. They receive all the knowledge they need as elementary students, and it's more authentically learned along the way. While Tracey could have had her students stick with more generic opinion-writing topics, investigating social issues allows students to write about ideas with deeper meanings and create a higher level of work with more relevance to their lives.

A higher level of work is one of the great benefits of this project. Students can also explore topics that may not impact their personal lives at that moment, but learning about them helps them to develop empathy for others. For example, one year, a third-grade boy chose to explore the gender wage gap and wrote about appreciating and respecting women. Students are learning to think about people other than themselves and practicing an often-consequential skill of speaking up for themselves and others. In Tracey's classroom, students begin learning early on that speaking up and activism do not look the same for every individual. It does not always mean picketing or protesting, and sometimes, it means writing a letter to the board of education. Her students did just that to advocate for their school district to recognize Indigenous People's Day.

An activism project ends with students convening in the classroom, which has been decorated with a United Nations theme, and they hold a Youth Summit. Tracey creates a book with all their writing. Students can create protest signs and buttons to accompany their work.

These projects resulted in action, in addition to the learning. For example, one year, a student wrote about taking care of the environment. Then, he met with his class and the principal and convinced them to use recess time to clean up their school, resulting in their entire grade engaged in a school clean-up to make their community better.

Tracey wants her students to know that they are not too young to make a difference and that their voices matter. As a teacher, she recognizes the importance and benefits of providing students with educational spaces to engage in discussion and learn about topics that affect their communities. She knows that in a perfect world, they wouldn't worry or think about these problems, but they are, they have questions, and they care about these issues. In preparation for these discussions, Tracey makes it a point to be transparent with her students' families. Starting at the Open House, when families can visit the classroom at the beginning of the school year to meet the teacher and learn about their class, Tracey lets families know that they will be discussing different topics, and it will be in a safe and kid-friendly way. Also, if a highly sensitive topic comes up, she reaches out directly to families. She views these teacher-family relationships as teamwork. Together, they are supporting children who may be curious or even worried but want to learn more and understand why things are the way they are.

One challenge she has faced is time and curricular expectations. However, Tracey takes the available opportunities to incorporate relevant, meaningful topics. For her, this looks like maximizing social-emotional learning time, swapping out books for ones that dive into more relevant topics, creating writing projects that expand students' critical consciousness, and even planning science activities that incorporate solving real-world issues. For example, during a force and motion unit, students had to be playground engineers. They discussed the fact that their playground was not very accessible to students in wheelchairs. She posed the question for inquiry, "How could the playground be set up to be more accessible?" Students then investigated low-cost elements that could be added to be more inclusive so students in wheelchairs could more easily access the playground. Changes like this allow Tracey to meet expectations while teaching students about the power of activism in the face of societal challenges and helping them understand that their identities, such as ability, race, and gender, will not hold them back from being empowered to make a difference. From an instructional lens, Tracey also recognizes that "We can miss out on opportunities to see students shine in ways that are authentic" when we don't allow flexibility and choice.

As a student, Tracey had a lot of positive school experiences and felt this made a difference for her. She recognizes the importance of providing students with powerful, positive connections and also knows that some students need more in order to engage with their school community. She believes that students must know it's okay to speak up and say what they need.

Outside of the classroom, Tracey lives these values. She is passionate about promoting student voice, especially among younger students, and encouraging student leadership. As an avid reader and author, she recognizes that this is not as apparent in books for upper elementary students. As she puts it, "Kids [books] don't always need to be fluffy. Kids want to talk about the world, and we don't give them enough credit." Accordingly, she makes it a point to ensure that values of inclusivity and cultural responsiveness are ingrained into the fiber of the classroom, and not just a lesson. "Honoring students as people helps them to acclimate and understand the world and makes it a more comfortable place to be in."

In addition to social-emotional benefits, inclusive curricula and responsive pedagogy also support academic achievement and engagement, and they help all students develop a deep critical consciousness. This Hack is not just about materials but also our methods of teaching, learning, and assessing. It also covers school culture and climate. A focus on inclusive curricula and responsive and sustaining pedagogy in all of these areas will offer students a multitude of ways to access what's being taught and to exhibit what they've learned.

By applying what we learn about our students and making intentional incremental changes to teaching, learning, and assessing, we can develop our practitioner capacity to take an asset-based, inclusive approach to educating students.

HACK 2

CREATE SUSTAINABLE STRUCTURES
DISTRIBUTE LEADERSHIP FOR ANTI-RACIST EFFORTS

*If you want to go quickly, go alone.
If you want to go far, go together.*
– AFRICAN PROVERB

THE PROBLEM: ONE PERSON CANNOT SUSTAIN ALL ANTI-RACIST EFFORTS

IN ANY SCHOOL, if you ask staff what they need most, you'll often hear some variation of "time" and "resources." Teachers work tirelessly to plan lessons, grade student work, manage student behaviors, and keep up with responsibilities that fall under "other duties as assigned." Similarly, administrators are also spread thin, balancing their obligations as instructional leaders and building managers. Finding the time to make foundational changes can be extremely difficult and often leads to a few people attempting to make a change because they believe in it, but they simply do not have the time, resources, or support to do so effectively. As a result, new goals founded on the desire to be an anti-racist institution can fail when there are too few people trying to lead the efforts in addition to their other duties. Not only is this unsustainable, but it also sends the message that anti-racism and equity are not true values.

While I will use words like initiative, efforts, and change, make no mistake—anti-racism itself is not an initiative but a core value and foundational lens for all we do. The actions taken to reflect and embed this value and belief into the heart of your school community may come in the form of new changes and initiatives, so we must gather support to make sustainable changes that will last well into the future. The attempt to shift culture and beliefs in a school is only the beginning of progress, and it will be a heavy lift, sometimes enough to lead to burnout if the responsibility is not shared. If we want progress to take root and have meaning to the school community, we must move forward together.

THE HACK: CREATE SUSTAINABLE STRUCTURES

Implementing changes to be more inclusive in a school cannot be the responsibility of one person; instead, it must be a team effort. Some districts and schools have a director of diversity, equity, and inclusion (DEI) or another version of this title. However, establishing this type of specialized position requires longer-term planning and budgetary dedication, which is why I suggest creating a committee. Plus, a director of DEI role still requires the support of other advocates for anti-racist changes to continue. Nonetheless, a core group of people who support and promote progress is instrumental for change. If this is a valued effort, many must carry the workload to attain the desired change.

> **ANTI-RACISM ITSELF IS NOT AN INITIATIVE BUT A CORE VALUE AND FOUNDATIONAL LENS FOR ALL WE DO.**

One way to begin making changes is to form a committee of people tasked with supporting these efforts in ways that meet the needs of the school. In some schools, this group is called the diversity, equity, and inclusion (DEI) committee, anti-racism committee, equity team, or another variation. The group could look different in any school environment based on factors such as size, resources, and goals of the school. It's also possible that your school does not have any structure for distributed leadership committees or teams, and you would need to start from scratch. However, once the committee is formed and titled, the goal is for this group to become a regular part of the school's structure, which allows for more consistency and follow-through. Creating a core group to expand change on a whole-school level is crucial to the sustainability of the effort and to making sure that staff is supported in their work.

Anti-racism is not a phase or a quick fix. It is a lens that allows us to see, acknowledge, and take steps toward dismantling systems and practices that deepen racial disparity between students, thus providing a path to educating students in a way that allows *all* of them to achieve success. Anti-racist teaching is what we want for our students. Creating structures that support this work in a sustainable way is the first step.

ANTI-RACIST TEACHING

WHAT YOU CAN DO TOMORROW

Forming a group to champion these efforts can be a big shift in your school community. It may even cause surprise, hesitation, pushback, or positive excitement. With so many different perspectives and opinions about what it means to be anti-racist, it is critical to move ahead with intention and purpose. To get ready for these different reactions and ensure a smooth start, here are ways to start preparing.

- **Look at your school's data.** Data is a key factor when trying to determine any direction and rationale for schoolwide endeavors. People in your school may already agree that anti-racist work is necessary, but some folks may need quantifiable data to understand why. Additionally, school data will help determine the areas that need the most support and where the school already has strengths. Information such as this helps you plan for more meaningful actions. Begin by analyzing data disaggregated by demographics:
    - behavior data such as referrals and suspensions
    - attendance data such as chronic absences and tardiness
    - academic achievement data such as standardized test scores

Create Sustainable Structures

- family, student, and teacher survey information about their experiences, such as a belonging survey (if this is not offered, consider adding it)
- graduation and dropout rates

As you analyze data sorted by demographics, look for disparities between demographic groups of students. For example, are certain racial groups consistently scoring higher or lower than other groups? How do English language learners' achievements compare to non-English language learners? If you have students receiving free or reduced lunch or financial aid in an independent school, how does their attendance data compare to others? Disparities in data can point to inequities and help us determine areas of need. Begin looking for this information on state, district, and school websites and, of course, talking with school administrators. If this data is not readily available, then pivot to brainstorming how you can gather it.

- **Talk with teachers.** If you are a teacher, an administrator, a coach, part of the support staff, or in any other role in a school, you know that relationships with colleagues are just as valuable as the relationships you build with students. Building relationships with staff where you can talk with them and develop an understanding of how they feel about anti-racism provides valuable information about how best to proceed and the pace you'll take. Of course, depending on your role, keep in mind that you may not get a completely honest answer from everyone for fear of being judged. That being said, prior to speaking with staff, make a list of what you want to learn from your conversations and create intentional questions around those items. Do you want to gain more insight about who could be a leader in these efforts? Are you interested in learning who will advocate for anti-racist efforts, even if they're not on the committee? Are you simply attempting to gauge general interest in being a part of the team? Talking to staff will also help you to recognize who understands the importance of anti-racism and how this manifests in their classrooms.

You may also learn who, if anyone, received training on related topics, such as culturally responsive teaching and restorative practices. People who have sought out opportunities to learn and grow are key individuals to lead by example and learn from. Getting an idea of who is already familiar with this work and who is not can absolutely inform the amount of support that staff needs. You will also want to strategically prioritize people with whom you know you want to speak. Since you probably don't have time to talk with every staff member, think about talking with teachers and staff from various perspectives to gain a wide range of opinions and examples.

- **Read and understand your district and school's mission and vision.** In preparation for building a rationale and purpose, consider what language your district and school are already using that you can utilize. You may find it on your school and district's website or in the handbook. Some schools and school systems explicitly state their anti-racist values, while others may not mention anything regarding race or culture. However, they likely talk about supporting student success, positive relationships, and the quality of instruction. All of this can be understood through an anti-racist lens, meaning that we pursue these goals in ways that intentionally address racism and bias. Even if you are in a system that openly states that it does not support anti-racist work, goals such as high student achievement, high-quality instruction, and positive relationships are strengthened when the school understands the impact of racism on their practices, policies, and programs and aims to dismantle barriers and evolve in their practice.
- **Learn about distributed leadership teams in education.** Forming a team is one step, but creating an environment that supports collaboration and productive activities to drive change is another. Understanding the hallmarks of a distributed leadership team that would make it successful, sustainable, and fruitful is essential to ensuring it can fulfill its purpose. For a short read about distributive

leadership, I recommend the article "Distributive Leadership in Schools: How to Develop DL Teams" by the Center for Student Achievement Solutions. For a more in-depth understanding, read "Meaningful and Sustainable School Improvement with Distributed Leadership" by Jonathan Supovitz, John D'Auria, and James Spillane. Take the time to learn about the foundations of a distributed leadership team and effective team norms and practices.

By accomplishing these tasks first, you can create a structure for implementation that best suits your school's needs, your time, and the resource limitations. As with any new initiative, you'll want to carefully plan how to most efficiently and effectively implement it.

A BLUEPRINT FOR FULL IMPLEMENTATION

Step 1: Determine who will be part of the group.

Your school may already have a structure for schoolwide teams, committees, or another way of distributing leadership. Whatever that structure is, a group of people leading anti-racist efforts allows for a more equitable way of implementing change so the responsibility does not fall on a single teacher or building administrator, especially if there is no standalone DEI position in your building. This structure also allows teachers' voices to be heard from the start and not as an afterthought.

The people who make up this team could be folks who are still learning about what anti-racism means and looks like, or they may already live this life in and outside of their classroom. More than likely, this group will be a mix, and that's okay. It adds value when efforts are led by a group with mixed perspectives and roles. However, all staff can hold a shared vision and understanding of why anti-racist work is needed in your school. When assembling this team, avoid making assumptions about who will want to be a part of it—especially if you are in a school (like many) where there are few teachers of color. It is vital to amplify the voices and center the perspectives of Black, Indigenous, and other people of color in anti-racist work and to be mindful that this does not mean expecting teachers of color to shoulder the weight of these efforts. For this reason, transparently talking with staff beforehand is such a valuable action.

Step 2: Determine the purpose of this group.

Among the many questions to consider, think about the following: Will the group lead schoolwide activities and possibly professional development? What resources are available? How will the school build the capacity of this group so they are prepared to implement changes as a legitimate and purposeful part of the school's infrastructure? The goals of this group heavily depend on the needs of your school and what has already been done regarding anti-racist work; the efforts that follow are to build the strengths of the school and support areas of growth. A vision and purpose will frame the group's effort moving forward. It's necessary for staff to understand the importance of this work by developing a clear picture of why anti-racist work is needed.

Start by collecting and analyzing data to determine school needs first, and then determine the next steps. Analyzing school data is a valuable way to determine the purpose and generate a shared understanding of why. The data could be about student achievement, climate and culture, teacher demographics and retention, and, importantly, anecdotal data that represents school community members, including students, staff, families, and other stakeholders such as community partners and board members. Look at data through a critical lens and analyze disparities between demographic groups. Data tells a story, and as educators, we must be honest and reflective about what the data shows. Using this information, the team can determine what will offer the best and most meaningful benefits to the school community.

Lastly, share communication with the school community so everyone knows about this team and what their work will involve.

Step 3: Determine when the team will convene.

To create a sustainable structure, one must consider when this group will have the chance to meet and plan. Are there already structures in place for when they can meet, such as professional learning community (PLC) opportunities and professional development (PD) occasions? How often can they consistently meet? Will they be provided with enough time to create a plan and carry it out? Finding times for the group to collaborate and meet during school hours is crucial for sustainability. You can also discuss the possibility of getting substitute coverage for classroom teachers and exploring your school or district guidelines around paying participants to meet after school. If it's reasonable, agreed to, and within staff contracts, common planning time is another time for the group to meet. Professional development days and PLC times are great occasions if they happen frequently enough. While many individuals are motivated to stay after school and use their personal time to meet, explore other options first out of respect for your team's expertise and time.

Step 4: Create and implement a Plan, Do, Study, Act (PDSA) cycle.

Once you establish a structure for the group to meet and collaborate, create a plan for the way ahead. One method you may choose to utilize is "Plan, Do, Study, Act," a cycle named by Walter Shewhart and William Edwards Deming that helps to ensure the longevity of your school's changes and establishes a way ahead for the future. (See Image 2.)

Prior to creating a plan, the team collects and analyzes data to uncover areas of disparity and understand staff mindsets, family perspectives, and student experiences. They may have already done this in Step 2. Next, they can determine a goal and create a "Plan," the first part of the PDSA cycle. What is the idea for change, and what do they want to see as a result? The plan the team sets could span the course of the school year, encompass multiple activities, and even be derived from a larger school or district goal. Additionally, it's crucial to determine how you will measure progress—how will you know the plan is successful? For example, if the group's long-term goal is to improve student behavior, they may create a plan to implement restorative practices. The plan could be written as, "If all faculty and staff implement restorative practices over the course of the school year to respond to student behaviors and build community, then the number of students receiving referrals and suspensions will decrease, and racial disparity in our behavior data will decrease." (For more about how to implement schoolwide restorative justice practices, read *Hacking School Discipline Together* by Jeffrey Benson.) As part of the plan, the group determines their timeline, how progress will be measured, and when to collect and analyze data.

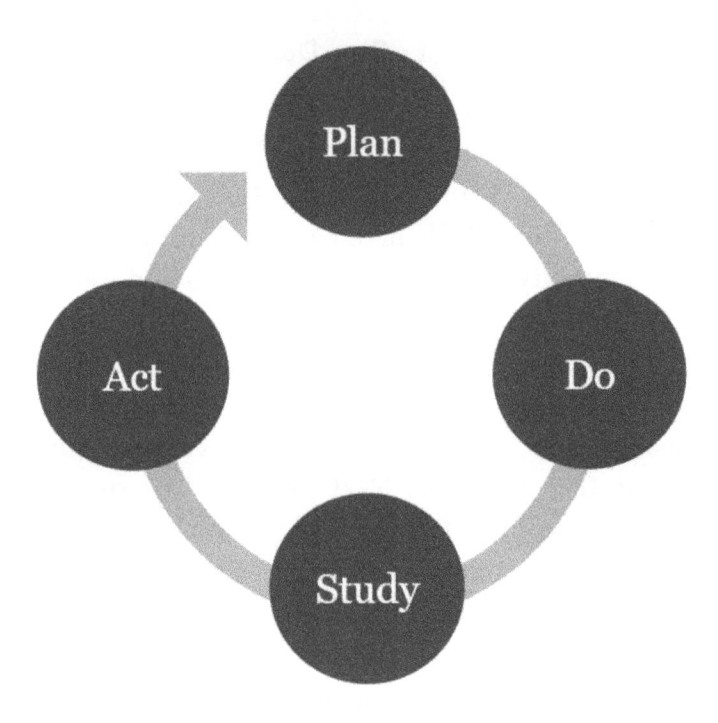

Image 2

Next, the group will move on to the "Do" part of the cycle. They must record what needs to happen to carry out the plan. With the previous example, the group might take these steps:

- provide professional learning about restorative practices over the school year
- teachers, administrators, and all adults will utilize strategies that align with restorative practices when addressing challenging student behavior and conflicts
- ask for and document adult and student feedback
- analyze referral and suspension data during the stated times
- continuously return to the "if ... then ..." hypothesis to check progress and pivot when necessary

The third part of this cycle is to "Study" the results of what has been done, then reflect and discuss what was learned. Based on the team's plan, there may be both qualitative and quantitative data to consider. Feedback and experiences are extremely valuable data, and one can reflect on them to determine the next step of the PDSA cycle, which is to "Act." The team will act in response to the results they studied. Here, honesty and transparency are critical. Consider what worked and what didn't during the "Do" part of the cycle, based on your data. Then decide how this learning will impact the next step. Will you adjust, adapt, or strategically abandon the original plan based on the results? How you "Act" in response to the results informs the ongoing iterations of the PDSA cycle and the future work to be done.

OVERCOMING PUSHBACK

Even though anti-racist education is an ideal that many educators strive toward and support, there are bound to be concerns and pushback as it becomes a schoolwide value. The following are common retorts you may hear about anti-racism education and practices. Whatever the pushback may be, believe in the power of listening and holding honest conversations. The end goal is unwavering, and understanding general concerns and misconceptions can help you formulate a more effective plan moving forward. Here are a few common concerns about this Hack and how to address them.

This work will be divisive; we don't need to focus on race. There's no denying that conversations about race can be challenging. That being said, there must be transparency with staff about the motives for doing this work. For hundreds of years in the United States, racism has been, and continues to be, used to subject people of color to inhumane and unfair treatment, further maintaining racial and socioeconomic disparity. It is unrealistic to think that the results of hundreds of years of racist thinking, practices, and laws simply disappeared when segregation was declared unlawful. Systemic racism still affects every area of society today. Detailed accounts and legal documentation support this observation. I highly recommend starting with the book *The Color of Law: A Forgotten History of How Our Government Segregated America* by Richard Rothstein (2017). In education, we see the impact when we look at the disparities in student achievement between racial groups, the racial segregation of schools and neighborhoods across the United States, the low numbers of teachers of color compared to white teachers, and even in the white-centric materials and resources that many students are taught from. We also know that racist beliefs and practices have been passed down from generation to generation. Even if it isn't explicitly discussed and named as racist, these beliefs about which race, skin tone, language, ethnicity, hair texture, vernacular, music, or behavior is superior, and the ways these beliefs are expressed through conscious and unconscious bias, absolutely still permeate every aspect of society to the detriment of students' success.

We cannot address racial injustices or harmful beliefs without taking intentional, thoughtful actions and making changes to systems that perpetuate racial discrimination. Your approach to introducing anti-racist work in your building, and possibly district, must be done with the utmost care and consideration. No matter how you start, it's possible to receive a barrage of disagreements, defensiveness, and anger. But stick with it. Teachers, who will likely participate in most of the training and activities, generally love their students and want the best for them. To provide the best educational environment, one must be willing to have courageous conversations that consider the experiences of all students and the influence of racism on and around us. We must be willing to have a growth mindset and be open to the possibility that we have personal work to do if we want to be better educators and human beings.

One way you can begin to understand how comfortable teachers around you are with this work is through building relationships. Again, this is why talking with staff improves outcomes. Take time to understand their encounters with race, their upbringing, and their points of view. The better you understand each person's perspective, the more effectively you can plan for future professional learning and other support. Develop an understanding of how to meet their needs so you can better serve students.

Our school doesn't need this. This pushback is especially common in schools with predominantly white students. However, anti-racist work is necessary for *all* students. Anti-racist practices and policies allow us to provide a more enriching and responsive environment and higher-quality instruction to support academic success. Students are also encouraged to develop a deeper sense of self. Anti-racist practices help students develop empathy for those around them and understand perspectives that are different from theirs. Hearing various viewpoints is especially critical for white students. To dismantle inequitable systems, white students must also become aware of their identities and biases to disrupt harmful thinking and beliefs. Anti-racist practices help students do that. Academically, these practices also help students from all racial backgrounds develop the skills to think critically, consider information and situations from multiple perspectives, and gain exposure to educational content from a diverse array of voices—all of which support their academic success.

> ANTI-RACIST PRACTICES HELP STUDENTS DEVELOP EMPATHY FOR THOSE AROUND THEM AND UNDERSTAND PERSPECTIVES THAT ARE DIFFERENT FROM THEIRS.

Another response to this pushback is to share information about racial disparities based on the data. Every student deserves to be successful. Even if BIPOC students account for less than 10 percent of your school population, their achievements and experiences matter. Carefully analyze data for disparities and root causes. Data tells a story. Carefully analyzing data over time reveals increases, decreases, growth, successes, consistent areas of challenge, and even points of celebration; utilizing this information to create a picture of your school may help staff understand why this work is necessary, especially if certain groups of the student population are consistently underperforming.

We don't have time to add more work to our day. While more time cannot be added to the day, delegation and collaboration are essential. Having a team to promote and lead efforts allows for a greater capacity to create schoolwide activities and shared resources. It is also a good first step to getting a handle on misconceptions around anti-racist work, as well as what some people believe are roadblocks to implementation. Teaching with an anti-racist lens does not necessarily mean that teachers must create completely new content. However, it should change the way we do things. Share this message with educators who offer this pushback.

Some concerns may be valid, and by knowing them early, the group can work together to consider how to address them. As the team paves the way ahead, they can share these goals and rationales with staff so they know what to expect, especially regarding what will be asked of them and how they will be supported by their colleagues, administration, and possibly district leadership. Sometimes, just knowing that our concerns have been taken into serious consideration helps to ease worries about new endeavors.

THE HACK IN ACTION

In 2021, our elementary school's Equity Committee met for the first time. The principal had tasked me with chairing the committee, which was composed of teachers across different grade levels and specialties. Some of them had already engaged in their own learning about racial equity, and some were new to these conversations. At the time, I was in graduate school, completing my administrative certification and learning about the importance of analyzing school and district climate, culture, and academic data, as well as continuous improvement cycles. My new awareness of the importance of creating goals based on data informed my decision to create a meeting agenda focused on these tasks:

1. Determine what data is available to create goals around and what data is still needed.

2. Determine the school's greatest strengths from which to build anti-racist work and areas that need to be supported based on school data.

3. Create goals that align with district equity work *and* meet the needs of the building.

Prior to the first Equity Committee meeting, I dug into some of the data I had already collected and met with the district's director of equity and instruction. From our conversations and knowing what the data showed about our school and district, I was able to gain a deeper understanding of what would be feasible for our committee to focus on. Although we would be meeting for an hour at scheduled PLC times throughout the year, time was limited. As teachers, all our plates were already full, so we had to create achievable and meaningful goals that met the needs of our school and district.

Fast forward to our first meeting: I immediately realized that while this committee had teachers at all stages of their personal learning about racial equity, we shared an understanding and commitment to creating goals and making changes that would create a positive environment for all students. Teachers on this committee brought a variety of perspectives and experiences, all of which helped us implement changes that were reflective of student and staff needs.

We created two goals around which we structured all follow-up activities, recommendations, and implementations.

> Goal 1: Increase awareness and involvement of families and students in relation to the school's focus on equity.
>
> Goal 2: Provide grade-level-appropriate, racial-equity-related lessons and resources to staff.

Based on the goals, actions we've taken since the creation of this committee include:

- create resource folders that staff have access to throughout the year that also highlight the celebration of heritage months
- plan schoolwide activities to celebrate heritage months
- create monthly equity newsletters for families to engage in conversations at home and highlight work happening in school
- organize a student club focused on racial equity
- make recommendations to the administration for engaging students, supporting staff, and involving families in our racial equity efforts

While working together as a committee, we accomplished many tasks and implemented activities that engaged students and staff. We also learned how to work together to make headway on our goals. We delegated tasks, helping us to share work that would otherwise be unmanageable for one person. Sharing the workload was especially crucial when it came to providing resources and planning activities.

Communication with the administration within our school and district was another vital element. Not only was it necessary for our work to support district equity goals, but it also allowed the committee to receive support when needed, gain a clearer understanding of why some of our ideas would or wouldn't be feasible, and connect with other schools in the district conducting similar work. Importantly, open communication between the committee and administrators established trust. If concerns or questions arose, they could be brought to everyone's attention, and we knew we had the support to pursue new ideas.

Of course, we also faced challenges and learned lessons along the way. After planning together, we often would still need to complete activities, like creating the newsletter or putting together resources, outside of our meeting time. However, this is why it was critical to have a sustainable structure for a committee. Having a schedule to plan together and delegate tasks cut down the time it would have taken to implement activities alone. Despite some imperfections, the existence of this committee and set meeting times gave us opportunities to tackle what we needed to address.

We also learned about the importance of flexibility. At different points in the school year and even across different school years, I realized that the capacity of staff to engage in activities varied depending on the climate at that time. We needed to be flexible with our timing of activities or actions to get maximum participation. Additionally, we had to be flexible in listening to each other. As I mentioned, this was a group containing varied perspectives, and we considered each point of view to plan the next steps that would meet the needs of students and take into account the varied experiences of staff. Our team's processes required a delicate balance of moving our equity work forward, no matter what, and being flexible in our pacing to get the greatest results.

As chair of the committee, I also noted the importance of staying on task. I don't mean this in the sense of conversation (having group norms helps with that) but in the larger task at hand—our committee's goals. Each time we met, I created an agenda. Our agenda would always be structured around our goals: reviewing new information or follow-ups, then continuing any planning or next steps from the previous meeting. Keeping this alignment and sustainable committee structure helped us build on previous work, keep track of our progress, ensure connection and relevance to our goals, and make the most of our time together.

Creating a group structure to support or begin anti-racist efforts is a key step in ensuring the sustainability of this work. Take the time to connect with staff and garner a genuine understanding of what is needed as you forge ahead. You may face pushback and challenges along the way; however, stick to the *why*. Providing students with equitable opportunities to be successful and removing barriers to that success are our *responsibility* as educators. By uniting voices to advocate for students and creating an environment where they are safe to advocate for themselves, we not only prepare them to be successful in our school building but in their communities and beyond.

HACK 3

FOSTER SHARED UNDERSTANDINGS
PLAN MEANINGFUL PROFESSIONAL LEARNING OPPORTUNITIES

> *The beauty of anti-racism is that you don't have to pretend to be free of racism to be anti-racist. Anti-racism is the commitment to fight racism wherever you find it, including in yourself. And it's the only way forward.*
> – IJEOMA OLUO, WRITER AND SPEAKER

THE PROBLEM: EDUCATORS NEED FOUNDATIONAL KNOWLEDGE TO SHIFT THEIR PRACTICES

WHILE PEOPLE HAVE hotly debated anti-racism and related topics, they often have to wade through a miasma of misinformation combined with a lack of true understanding about what anti-racism is. In schools, it cannot be assumed that educators know what anti-racism means or looks like when discussing anti-racist teaching. If we seek to create an environment that promotes anti-racist teaching without providing opportunities to develop a shared understanding and professional capacity, then we are setting up staff for confusion, frustration, and superficial efforts. Without providing authentic, meaningful professional learning about anti-racism and teaching, we risk creating a culture wherein simply adding a few new diverse texts and celebrating Black History Month are seen as enough to qualify as valuing diversity and being culturally responsive. They are not.

While these attempts may be well-intentioned, they are not enough to make authentic, lasting changes. Diverse literature and celebrating heritage months are valuable ways to create identity-affirming spaces that provide "windows and mirrors" to students. On their own, however, they will not shift mindsets and practices predicated on racist beliefs that harm students. While educators may be willing to evolve in their practices and engage in learning, a schoolwide shift toward anti-racism cannot happen without developing a deeper shared understanding of anti-racist teaching through professional learning.

THE HACK: FOSTER SHARED UNDERSTANDINGS

It is not enough to state that anti-racism is necessary. While many educators agree and accept that it is wrong for students to be faced with inequitable opportunities for achievement, they may not know what it means to teach with an anti-racist lens or what professional work is involved to get there. For this reason, we must foster a shared understanding of knowledge, practices, and values through professional learning.

> **WHILE EDUCATORS MAY BE WILLING TO EVOLVE IN THEIR PRACTICES AND ENGAGE IN LEARNING, A SCHOOLWIDE SHIFT TOWARD ANTI-RACISM CANNOT HAPPEN WITHOUT DEVELOPING A DEEPER SHARED UNDERSTANDING OF ANTI-RACIST TEACHING THROUGH PROFESSIONAL LEARNING.**

Through high-quality professional learning, staff can begin or continue to develop their understanding of anti-racism and what this looks like in their school and classroom. By leveraging the knowledge of folks already engaged in this work, such as the committee formed in Hack 2, and centering the experiences of staff, students, and families of color, schools create authentic opportunities for staff to gain a deeper understanding of the value and purpose of anti-racism. Since anti-racist teaching and learning involves shifting our mindset and beliefs and a multitude of practices, we must authentically center it as a community value and foundation for everything else. When done well, professional learning is a vital tool to support the belief that anti-racism and racial equity are not just hot discussion items but true values in the school community.

Developing a shared understanding through professional development also provides everyone who works in the school with intentional time to dive into the self-reflection we need to make changes to our thinking and beliefs. As participants' self-awareness progresses through meaningful reflective activities, we can make clearer connections between the intersectionality of our own identities and our relationships with students and educational practices. Then, we can engage in professional learning that provides the knowledge we need to develop or strengthen our anti-racist lens to evolve our practices. Our knowledge can include content-based information and build a foundation of understanding about racial inequity within the context of education and anti-racist practices to combat it. This development of learning helps participants understand how racism affects students' well-being and academic achievement, as well as why this learning is relevant to educators. A critical piece of this, however, is consistency. Professional learning cannot be a one-and-done event. If you are part of a larger school district that is leading these efforts, then your school has the responsibility to continue providing ways for educators to engage in reflection and exploration of anti-racist work.

A progression of developing a shared understanding through professional learning and providing time for educators to make connections about why they need this work will help them recognize what personal growth they need. By building a strong foundation of "why," allowing adult learners to make relevant connections to their lives, and steadily developing knowledge about anti-racist practices, you will support educators in developing the lens and practices they need to make a powerful and positive impact on their students' engagement and achievement in school.

WHAT YOU CAN DO TOMORROW

If there's anything that educators hate, it's professional development that wastes time that could be spent on planning, prepping, grading, or the many other tasks they need to do. Take time to thoroughly plan out your next steps to provide meaningful, relevant professional learning. As you plan, here are five actions you can take in the short term to prepare:

- **Strengthen your knowledge.** Whether you lead this work or support it, build your knowledge about equity, anti-racism, the history of race in your location, and movements for justice. Additionally, as leaders or those facilitating conversations about anti-racism, you can always engage in the personal work of recognizing and deconstructing your conscious and unconscious biases. As educators supporting other educators in learning, that can often elicit emotional responses, and you must lead by example and model what it looks like to be vulnerable enough to engage in a mindset of self-work and growth. Strengthen your knowledge by:
    - reading books and articles, listening to podcasts, and watching films about race and equity
    - joining organizations and meeting with other educators to engage in social justice work
    - seeking stories that amplify the voices and experiences of marginalized populations
- **Look at your school's data and review the PDSA cycle.** Review the PDSA cycle that was created in Hack 2, and consider what professional learning opportunities will best support those plans and goals. The efforts that happen next through professional learning are part of the "Do" step of the PDSA cycle and support the school's progress toward its goals. Regularly reviewing these goals

and the plan will also help to keep the team's work focused and purposeful.

- **Check in with staff.** Discussing race can be heavy for all involved. For educators of color, it can be emotionally challenging to talk about their encounters with racism and unpack internalized racist ideologies, especially if they are in a mostly white school. For white educators, it may be difficult to recognize, admit, and unpack their own racial biases and their roots. School leaders and those organizing the professional learning create better outcomes when they take the time to build trust and check in with individual staff members before and after sessions to give specific attention to what they are anxious about going in and their experiences during the training. Having these personal "check-ins" may call attention to underlying issues as well as care for the emotional well-being of staff. Moreover, as mentioned before, when discussing race, individual teachers and larger committees are likely to face pushback. Gaining a deeper understanding of the root causes of frustration means you will have a better idea of how to provide support. Engaging in anti-racist professional learning is not voluntary; making it mandatory will help you figure out what additional support you need for staff who disengage or go on the defensive.
- **Cultivate leadership among future facilitators and advocates.** If people are already in your building who teach and learn through an

anti-racist lens, connect with them first. You might find that they are supportive of these efforts and willing to help move things forward with their talents and expertise. Spend time providing support and resources for these individuals to become strong leaders. School leaders can do this by offering professional learning specifically for facilitators. They can also share and fund opportunities outside of school, such as conferences and workshops, for them to collaborate with likeminded educators. In addition to supporting these educators in their leadership growth, it is an investment for students.

- **Learn about andragogy, or Adult Learning Theory, developed by Malcolm Knowles.** Andragogy is the study of adult education, as opposed to pedagogy, which specifically concerns how children learn. If you are planning, facilitating, or leading any format of adult learning, such as professional learning sessions, it is worthwhile to gain a deeper understanding of how adults learn. Unfortunately, many educators have had to suffer through countless "sit and get" professional development, which means school committees and administrative teams might have an uphill battle with buy-in. While it may take more time and resources to thoughtfully plan professional learning that does not solely rely on lecturing, there is power in curating meaningful activities that call on the perspectives of the learners,

> allow time and space for them to construct their own meaning, differentiate for the needs of each learner, and make clear the purpose and relevance to their daily work. By becoming familiar with Adult Learning Theory, you will design more high-quality, effective professional learning opportunities.

A BLUEPRINT FOR FULL IMPLEMENTATION

Step 1: Determine why, what, who, where, and when for each learning session.

Taking the time to plan is a critical first step to facilitating any professional learning. Plan intentionally and with a goal in mind. You also want to understand what prior training staff have engaged in and whether they can or should be connected to your work. Here are factors to consider every time you plan professional learning around anti-racism.

- *Why:* Sometimes, we assume that adult learners already know the purpose of what they're doing, but facilitators need to be clear. If precious time is taken to develop their capacity about a subject, they deserve a clear and relevant explanation as to why. Whether or not everyone agrees on the same "why" is a different story. However, if the "why" is clear and the connection is drawn to their daily work, learning becomes more relevant, meaningful, and worthwhile.
- *What:* During your planning process, develop a clear written objective for the learning session. It's a good practice to guide the direction you want to go. Just

as teachers may have a learning target so they know what they want students to gain from a lesson, be clear about what you want to accomplish in the time educators spend together. The goal you set will depend on the needs of your school, and examples include:

- Educators will reflect on their own cultural lens to unpack how biases may shape their perspective regarding students.
- Educators will learn about the ways that identity is connected to relationships with students, and they will learn strategies to develop authentic connections.
- Educators will learn instructional strategies to teach in ways that are culturally responsive, relevant, and sustaining.

Then, when creating materials to share with staff, provide some form of a blueprint, map, or agenda about how they will spend their time and where it falls in the larger context of the goal. Doing so will help participants prepare mentally and even physically for what's to come. Oftentimes, professional learning takes place at the end of a long, stressful day. It is helpful to be able to mentally prepare if you know you will actively participate in conversations and activities that require engagement versus a lecture or "sit and get" form of professional learning. Additionally, it helps build an understanding and connect learning if you know where you're going and how you're getting there.

- *Who:* Know your audience. Who will be present for the session? What is their history with this topic? What are their particular needs and strengths? Knowing if this session will introduce new content or continue ongoing conversations will inform what you plan to do and how you'll do it. It's also helpful to know if allies and advocates will be in the room and who they are. Also, consider if any participants are disengaged, distract others, or seek to derail the work. Knowing your audience will help you to plan for the most productive seating and engagement.

- *Where* and *when:* These are obvious logistics to consider when planning professional learning, but do not take them lightly. Be intentional when planning where the learning will take place.
  - ▶ Is the seating conducive for group discussion?
  - ▶ Is the lighting adequate?
  - ▶ Will there be distracting noises?
  - ▶ Are there connections for technology?
  - ▶ Is there an internet connection for attendees to get online if needed?
  - ▶ Is it a comfortable temperature, or will people need to leave the room to warm up or cool down?

All these questions are valuable! Of course, space may be limited, but try to create an environment that is comfortable for learning. Equally, if you have options for when professional learning takes place, consider when staff will have sufficient time to discuss and engage with the material. Or, if you know time is limited, plan activities with this in mind. If you are planning professional learning that will last longer than an hour, include breaks. Additionally, always consider the time of year. All year can be stressful for teachers, but key times are extra busy. So be mindful about when you plan for certain topics and activities if you want the most engagement and to ensure they meet the most prevalent needs at the moment.

As you plan, remember that often, teachers of color are unintentionally (and sometimes intentionally) handed the burden of being *expected* to teach white colleagues about race and racism. However, when this role is assigned because we are BIPOC, and often without our consent, it overlooks the fact that we wrestle with our own racial trauma and may not have the bandwidth to navigate everyone else's learning and processing, too. As you prepare for or continue with professional learning, prioritize the viewpoints and safety of staff of color to ensure this will also be a fruitful practice for them and not cause more unintentional harm. Facilitators can plan activities that require everyone to participate and share examples, not only the staff of color, as they do not serve as a representation of an entire community, nor should they bear that responsibility.

Step 2: Start with self-awareness.

Before diving into specific practices to employ in the classroom, educators benefit from engaging in what Dr. Dena Simmons calls vigilant self-awareness, meaning that educators benefit by spending time learning about their own identities, the intersectionality of these identities, and how they shape experiences of power, privilege, and discrimination. Taking time to unpack their positionality will help educators recognize their perspectives, biases, and deeply held beliefs that inform how they interact with the world, especially with their students. It is critical to provide opportunities to unpack implicit biases and how they inform everything from instructional materials, rules around behavior, expectations for family involvement, and every other aspect of schooling. Everyone has implicit biases about race because of our personal experiences, upbringing, media, and societal culture; we all have internalized positive and negative messages about racial groups and other identities. By taking time to engage in deep self-reflection, educators will draw clearer connections to how this influences their work and what needs to change to provide a more equitable and enriching education for all students. The action steps after engaging in vigilant self-awareness, according to Dr. Simmons in her article "How to Be an Antiracist Educator," are:

- acknowledge racism and the ideology of white supremacy
- study and teach representative history
- talk about race with students
- when you see racism, do something

> **EVERYONE HAS IMPLICIT BIASES ABOUT RACE BECAUSE OF OUR PERSONAL EXPERIENCES, UPBRINGING, MEDIA, AND SOCIETAL CULTURE.**

Step 3: Plan learning that connects experience to practice.

Your next step for developing a shared understanding among staff is to build their capacity to recognize and change practices. Provide professional development about practices that support teaching and learning, building relationships, and classroom management through an anti-racist lens. The learning will be ongoing and include how to apply new knowledge, practices, and strategies within the school and classrooms. At each step or introduction to a different practice, strategy, or way of understanding, support educators in making clear connections to how it could look in their working context. In other words, always strive to answer the questions of "What does this look like in the classroom?" and "Why is it good for students?" During each session, provide time for staff to collaborate with one another to discuss how they can implement their new learning. Following professional learning, provide educators with ongoing support and resources to implement.

Here is a list of strategies, practices, and topics for professional learning:

- culturally responsive, relevant, sustaining practices
- restorative practices and relationship-building practices that support behavior management
- microaggressions, macroaggressions, and bias
- identity development and deep self-reflection
- intersectionality and positionality
- social justice issues
- the historical and political impact of race and racism
- questioning for critical thinking
- diverse children's literature
- analyzing curriculum and materials for bias
- connecting with families and the larger community
- linguistic diversity
- instructional practices for student-centered learning

Step 4: Debrief and revise.

As you support staff through professional learning sessions, continually request, review, and apply feedback. Perfection doesn't exist, but practice makes progress. Save at least five to ten minutes before the end of a session to collect feedback. In the days after a session, check in with trusted staff members to hear their honest feedback. Whether good or bad, feedback will help you understand what worked well, what didn't, and what knowledge staff may need more or less of. This information is extremely valuable in helping you plan more effective learning times that truly meet the needs of the participants.

OVERCOMING PUSHBACK

Learning new ideas and practices can be exciting, but learning information that makes us question everything both internally and externally can be uncomfortable. However, this helps us to grow. Below are potential responses to educators who may have a hard time understanding the "why" behind engaging in learning that might make them feel guilt or anger. However, if these educators intend to remain in classrooms, then it should be a nonnegotiable expectation to move forward as lead learners and model the expectation of growth that we place on students.

We don't have problems with racism in my classroom. When looking for signs of racism, some people expect to see explicit offenses. However, educators must also understand that racism is often subtle and indirect, such as in the form of microaggressions. According to Dr. Derald Wing Sue, "Microaggressions are the everyday verbal, nonverbal, and environmental slights, snubs, or insults, whether intentional or unintentional, which communicate hostile, derogatory, or negative messages to target people based solely upon their marginalized group membership." For example, a common microaggression I endured growing up was being told I sounded "white" by peers, and simultaneously being told I was "well spoken" and "articulate" by white adults. These statements communicated a negative message that if I were to sound Black or use African American Vernacular English (AAVE), I would not be well-spoken or articulate. While not stated explicitly, the implicit message I learned was that to sound intelligent, I had to sound white. Teaching about microaggressions through professional learning helps educators understand the many ways that racism can show up in the classroom, such as via comments that they may think are complimentary or harmless. Among many actions, this includes the treatment of students, the way we address and interpret behavior, grading practices, and the way different races are represented in our classrooms through materials and resources.

Many Black, Indigenous, and other people of color can recall encounters with racism in the early stages of childhood from both teachers and peers. As educators, even if you, coworkers, or students are not making blatantly racist comments that you are aware of, it does not mean that racism is nonexistent. If educators do not engage in work around their own biases and beliefs, or intentionally take action to create more inclusive classrooms, they are likely perpetuating racist ideologies whether they intend to or not because of their own implicit biases and beliefs that they may have grown up thinking were not problematic. But, as we learn, we can do better.

I'm here to teach; leave politics about race out of it. Teachers who strive to create equitable classrooms and provide the support that students need to thrive must recognize the politics, laws, and beliefs that have negatively affected historically marginalized groups. Through professional learning, you can facilitate education about the historical and political context of racism and how it connects to your community and students. Regardless of personal political views, educators must be willing to grow and do what is best for students, with special consideration for those who have been historically marginalized. Engaging in professional development is not about politics, but it's the expectation of the job and what is best for *all* students.

Teachers are lead learners within their classrooms, and as aspects of their instructional content change or are updated, they must enhance their professional knowledge to meet the changes within their classrooms. Anti-racist work is no different. It is educators' professional duty to take responsibility for the part they play in how racism impacts students and what they can do about it. Whether or not the political debates of the day are promoting or suppressing conversations about race, doing what is best for students remains the priority. Additionally, there will likely be individuals who do not believe anti-racism belongs in school. While they are entitled to their opinion, if an educator is not willing to develop their understanding about race and how it affects their students, or to grow in their capacity to address racism in their classroom, then they do not belong in a classroom. That being said, they are in the classroom, and we can put policies in place that help us meet adults where they are and work toward meeting the needs of students.

I don't see my students' race; I treat them equally. To not see people's race or to be "colorblind" is to ignore the racism and oppression that BIPOC have faced and to disregard how these encounters have impacted people and communities. How can one build authentic relationships with students, create an affirming environment, or provide support that acknowledges the challenges they have or might face without seeing them holistically—which includes their racial identity? While "colorblindness" is often the belief of people who may intend no harm, it is harmful to disregard racial trauma and how racism and racialized experiences shape the lives of BIPOC. Often, this point of view stems from a lack of self-reflection regarding personal beliefs and biases, wanting instead to disengage from potentially uncomfortable conversations about race. Beginning professional development with deep self-reflection and learning about implicit bias is so critical.

Another tool that is meaningful when explaining to teachers why we all must engage in professional learning about anti-racism is to share real (and anonymous) stories and anecdotes about students' encounters with race in their classrooms and schools. Hearing about students' experiences with racism can bring awareness to educators and help them develop a sense of empathy and understanding as to why this work is necessary for their classrooms and schools. Of course, we must give the utmost care to students' anonymity and safety as they share their stories.

THE HACK IN ACTION

In August 2020, I was asked to create and facilitate one of the professional learning sessions for teachers that would take place before students returned to the building for the new school year. The session would focus on teaching with an anti-racist lens and specific strategies and practices teachers can use in the classroom. Before planning activities and resources to share, I took some time to think about a few key questions:

1. What did I want teachers to take away from the session?
2. What skills, perspectives, and statistics did they need from the session to teach with an anti-racist lens?
3. What foundational shared understanding would they need to move forward during and after the session?
4. How could I make their time in this virtual session engaging, relevant, and useful?
5. What relevant data did I have to guide any of my decisions?
6. How does the current social and political racial climate impact staff and this session?

Importantly, this virtual session took place during the COVID-19 pandemic and followed a summer of global protests and activism in response to police brutality and the murder of a Black man, George Floyd, by a white police officer.

Considering all these questions, I decided that before beginning any conversation, we needed to acknowledge the obvious, which meant addressing the history of racism on today's reality and the current movements for justice, drawing a clear line to how this hurts students and presenting clear and irrefutable evidence of racial disparity within our school's academic data. Such an introduction provided a shared foundational understanding of why we needed to engage in anti-racist teaching and the direct connection to our students. I also wanted to address what people might think and question before it caused disengagement and distraction. While some people still may have disagreed with the purpose and topic of my professional development, providing a clear explanation as to why this work was relevant and necessary at this time was crucial.

Next, I developed an agenda to structure how we would spend the session time. I created a detailed version for myself as the facilitator, and I revised it as I created the presentation and materials and a shorter outline to share with staff. I also determined the group norms to create a space conducive to productive discussion and participation. I planned to share these norms with the group and welcome feedback for revisions or additions before agreeing to them. After determining these routine details, I began to think more about questions 2 and 3:

- What skills, perspectives, and statistics did they need from the session to teach with an anti-racist lens?

- What foundational shared understanding would they need to move forward during and after the session?

Since this was our first time engaging in anti-racist work together, I decided to share key definitions so we'd have a common language, a general framework of what we needed to do to strengthen our anti-racist lens, and a specific explanation of where we would start within this framework, and why. As I planned, I thought carefully about what we could feasibly engage in during our time together so that teachers would walk away with the following:

1. Questions about how their identity influences who they are as teachers (this would be the start of a conversation for many; thus, I set a realistic expectation of walking away with more questions than answers)

2. A burgeoning understanding of anti-racist teaching and bias

3. Specific practices and strategies they could attempt in the classroom

The first activity staff engaged in was to unpack their identities. Participants completed the Social and Personal Identity Wheels adapted from "Voices of Discovery," Intergroup Relations Center, Arizona State University. We started by looking inward and reflecting on who we were. These reflections then helped us understand our privileges as well as our experiences with oppression due to certain identities we hold. Along with this personal reflection, participants engaged in group conversations to discuss how these identities shaped our beliefs, perceptions of others, and biases.

Next, I wanted the staff to learn about implicit bias, so rather than listening to me explain this, I looked for an engaging video to show what implicit bias is and how it influences us. With this new information, staff would then return to the initial identity activity and use the new shared understanding of biases to discuss how their identities shape their implicit biases. Realistically, I knew that staff would not walk away after one session unpacking all their biases, but I wanted to begin questioning their biases and stretching their thinking about how they affect their roles as educators. As I planned, I considered the different levels of understanding among staff. I knew that some people had already been engaging in anti-racist work, while for many others, this would be brand new. As a facilitator, I wanted a balance of activities that would inspire those who have already been engaging in anti-bias and anti-racist work to reflect and grow, as well as those who needed a supportive push forward.

After developing some form of understanding about our identities and implicit biases and considering how they affect our work as educators, I wanted to provide relevant tools that were applicable in the classroom. Having spent much time in many professional development sessions, I knew staff needed to walk away with actions they could immediately apply to their work. The application following professional learning is where students reap the benefits of teachers improving their professional practice. Therefore, I decided to engage staff in learning about the "Eight Competencies for Culturally Responsive Teaching" developed by New America through research on culturally relevant, responsive, and sustaining pedagogies. The eight competencies are:

1. Reflect on how one's own cultural lens, biases, values, and assumptions affect their teaching.

2. Recognize and redress bias in institutions and society.

3. Draw on students' cultures to shape curriculum and instruction, allowing them to connect their personal beliefs, values, and experiences to learning outcomes.

4. Bring real-world issues into the classroom.

5. Model high expectations for all students.

6. Promote respect for student differences.

7. Collaborate with families and the local community.

8. Communicate in linguistically and culturally responsive ways.

Rather than simply listing off the competencies, I created a visual that included specific ways staff could apply them. Finally, encouraging them to apply this learning was crucial, as was allocating time for participants to apply their learning in a space where they could ask questions, collaborate, and walk away having completed or started something useful. In my plans, I included pre-session instructions for K–5 staff to have the first English language arts lesson and text of the first unit on hand for this session. Then, I created a set of prompts to help them closely analyze the lesson and plan ways to refine or revamp it based on the Eight Competencies. Special education staff, specialists, and other support services would also have prompts to apply to their work so that everyone had a meaningful task to engage in.

Before letting the group start, I made a note to circle back to our focus of the day, anti-racist teaching, and that we wanted to apply our new understanding of bias when analyzing existing lessons and materials. Staff would also have a digital platform shared with them so that each grade level or group working together would be able to post their thoughts and key takeaways from their discussion. Not only would this give me an idea of each group's engagement and general perceptions of what they learned, but it would also serve as a resource that anyone could return to.

When they returned from their groups, we asked staff to share key takeaways from their discussion. I considered what next steps we could take to continue growing and applying the learning. I also included time for participants to share with me what they felt the next steps for our school would include, and I added their ideas to the shared presentation. It was a way for staff to advocate for what they needed to continue with this work and to make this a shared effort and hold us accountable to one another.

The final step, and one of the most important, was collecting feedback. I decided to use a digital survey so multiple parties could more easily access the comments. Staff would also have the option to complete their survey anonymously. I wanted real, honest feedback. After the surveys were submitted, I noted that about half of the staff did submit anonymously. The survey was a critical tool to inform future steps and provide administration and future facilitators with valuable information about what staff felt they needed. As part of my planning, I also created a bank of resources and linked many of them throughout the digital presentation. All of this would be shared with staff after the professional learning session. I wanted staff to have easily accessible resources to independently build on what we started together in the session.

Developing a shared understanding of what anti-racism is and looks like in education is crucial for your staff. They need time and space to dive into self-reflection, ask questions, and make sense of how they can apply new information as self-directed adult learners. By carefully planning for professional learning opportunities that offer this time and space, you will help them develop the skills and mindset to become anti-racist practitioners. As you plan and engage in professional learning together, be prepared for pushback. Take this as feedback to better understand how to support your staff's growth. It is critical that we push people past their comfort zone and be willing to interrogate problematic beliefs and assumptions. Developing the capacity to implement anti-racist practices may not be an easy journey, but the challenge is worth it if we want to do what is best for students.

HACK 4

PROVIDE ONGOING SUPPORT
OFFER TEACHERS PERSONALIZED AND WHOLE-SCHOOL SUPPORT

> *Be not afraid of discomfort. If you can't put yourself in a situation where you are uncomfortable, then you will never grow. You will never change. You'll never learn.*
> – JASON REYNOLDS, AUTHOR

THE PROBLEM: AUTHENTIC CHANGES DON'T OCCUR UNLESS STAFF HAS ONGOING SUPPORT

IF TEACHERS DO not receive continued support in the classroom after professional development about anti-racist practices, then efforts to build capacity can fail. Looking inward and learning what to do differently are the first steps; tangible change happens when educators turn their reflections into actions and applied learning in the classroom. These actions are where we get to see the impact on students, including in the areas of academics, relationships, behaviors, personal connections, and engagement. Without follow-up support, it's easy to continue maintaining the status quo, which has historically meant centering white students' experiences and not considering systemic racism—whether intentional or not.

Additionally, as educators engage in learning, some may think they're doing what they have been asked, but without the right support, follow-through, or understanding, their actions can be harmful and offensive. Blind compliance, no matter how well-intentioned, can be dangerous if we place new expectations on educators without the guidance and support they deserve. Anti-racism is not about "checking boxes" but about making authentic changes that address educational injustice. Without ongoing guidance beyond professional development sessions, teachers may struggle to apply new practices and integrate new knowledge in the classroom. Frustration due to a lack of support can also lead to the abandonment of learning, even from teachers who were willing to attempt new ways of doing things. Ongoing support is critical for progress.

> ANTI-RACISM IS NOT ABOUT "CHECKING BOXES" BUT ABOUT MAKING AUTHENTIC CHANGES THAT ADDRESS EDUCATIONAL INJUSTICE.

THE HACK: PROVIDE ONGOING SUPPORT

Continued support beyond professional development helps educators make the connections between educational theory and their learnings to practice and action. Through guidance in the classroom, such as providing resources, coaching, soliciting or offering feedback, and other support that directly addresses the work educators do with students, you will help teachers develop their practice as anti-racist educators and apply their learning to the daily situations they face.

As with any new learning, the most powerful moments are when we apply it to real-life situations. Being able to see how they can use new knowledge to solve a present problem is also what helps adult learners see the value in the knowledge and remain motivated to stay on the journey of change. Making shifts in teaching and behavior management practices can be difficult. If teachers have support available to them as they face challenges, the changes will be more manageable. Since anti-racism requires us to analyze and question our personal beliefs, as well as interrogate our daily thoughts and actions, this makes the journey even more complicated and emotionally charged.

Receiving support along this journey helps educators to embrace change and see the benefits for themselves and their students. While supports should be in place for everyone to move the school forward, individual encouragement can be more personalized, depending on what each educator and classroom needs. By providing this level of individualized support, teachers who are just beginning to understand anti-racism and teachers who are already successful anti-racist educators will all continue to grow. While whole-school support could mean offering resources for students and staff, individual support might include specific feedback connected to goals around culturally responsive teaching and individualized coaching.

Whether personal or generalized, ongoing support to teachers in their element makes a significant difference in growth and implementation. By making learning applicable after professional development, you can work to avoid abandonment, extreme frustration, and performative or offensive actions. Change takes time, and it is difficult to shift from the way we've always done something. However, investing time and effort to continually support teachers in developing their anti-racist practices is necessary for students' well-being .

> ### WHAT YOU CAN DO TOMORROW
>
> As with any endeavor, good planning is essential for effectiveness. You can take key actions now to provide educators with the most relevant and meaningful support. Changing pedagogical practices and shifting school culture and values are challenging. Yet, by understanding the needs of educators and providing support along the way, you will make the change more manageable and help staff see the value of their efforts.
>
> - **Return to the "Do" part of the PDSA cycle you created in Hack 2.** After facilitating professional learning connected to your school's needs, now you must provide the support that continues to meet those needs. The support that you determine is best for staff will directly impact their capacity to implement actions and changes that will meet the set goals. Review what you outlined in the PDSA plan to help you and your team stay on track, while also reflecting on what you have accomplished and what you still need to do.
> - **Consult with those leading the efforts.** As mentioned, the team or committee might be made up of people who are proficient as anti-racist educators or are still learning how to shift their practices.

Either way, these teachers can provide valuable insight as to what their colleagues are feeling and experiencing following professional learning. You can also call on them to inform the next steps for ongoing support. If they are teachers who feel confident as anti-racist educators, learn more about their learning journey and what helped them, as well as what supports and challenges they experienced along the way. For teachers who are still early in their learning, it would be valuable to know what supports they feel they'd benefit from and what aspects of the learning challenge them the most.

- **Visit classrooms.** The best way to know what's happening in classrooms is to get inside them. Visiting classrooms after teachers have engaged in professional learning can give you a good idea about their areas of strength and where they need continued support. Before visiting, hopefully, you already established a practice of being visible and developing trust among students and staff. Staff need not feel like visits or walkthroughs are "gotcha moments" or evaluations. Additionally, you'll want to know what you're looking for when visiting. For example, if teachers have learned about restorative practices, you might pay closer attention to classroom relationships and how the teacher and students respond to behavior in the classroom. After leaving, take time to consider what you've observed and how it informs the next steps. If you have not engaged in walkthroughs before, take time to learn how to make them beneficial for both the teacher and the visitor. To start your learning about walkthroughs, read "5 Best Practices for Classroom Walkthroughs" by Jason Cochran for a brief overview. According to Cochran, ideal walkthroughs are:

- informal
- no longer than about ten minutes
- non-evaluative and nonjudgmental
- focused on teacher development, not conformity
- part of a reflective dialogue process

To learn how a principal implemented walkthroughs, read "'Feedback Is Love:' Meaningful Classroom Walkthroughs" by Ben Klompus.

- **Connect with other educators engaged in social justice work.** Connection is a powerful way to learn from others and gain insights into the ongoing supports that have helped schools implement anti-racist practices. Whether through book clubs, social justice organizations, social justice-oriented events and conferences, social media groups, or trusted groups of educators from other schools—communicating with other anti-racist educators can give you more ideas about effective ways to support teachers. Visit symonejamesabiola.com for a list of organizations to connect with.

A BLUEPRINT FOR FULL IMPLEMENTATION

Step 1: Establish a process to collect feedback.

The support you provide to staff has to be relevant and meaningful to their work. In addition to utilizing data and aligning with school goals, you also want to hear directly from staff. What challenges are they facing? What support would they appreciate? What practices do they feel confident about? What surprised them as they implemented different practices? These are a few questions you could ask to help guide decisions about the support teachers need. You can collect this information in many ways. You can choose to intentionally share out a survey at different times of the year or after professional learning. You might also take the time to connect personally with staff members and ask the committee to reach out to colleagues. However you do it, consider methods to help you get the most accurate ideas of what staff needs to make real progress.

> **INVESTING TIME AND EFFORT TO CONTINUALLY SUPPORT TEACHERS IN DEVELOPING THEIR ANTI-RACIST PRACTICES IS A NECESSARY INVESTMENT IN STUDENTS' WELL-BEING.**

Step 2: Provide resources.

Providing staff and students with various resources is extremely helpful. The lack of time to search for resources, or funds to buy them, is often given as a reason for not incorporating more diverse instructional materials. Remove that barrier by providing grade-level-appropriate books and other learning materials to educators. Also, consider offering adult learning resources such as websites, helpful social media accounts, books, and articles for those who have questions and want to learn more but aren't sure where to go or who to ask. Sharing diverse materials for lessons, schoolwide events, and activities is also beneficial. The materials could be for content-area lessons and broken down by grade level. They could celebrate heritage months, holiday resources, and events such as Read Across America. Offering readily available resources also encourages teachers to incorporate diverse voices and perspectives in their classrooms year-round.

Step 3: Provide coaching and encourage mentorship.

It's common for schools to have coaching for academic subjects and behavior management. If you have academic coaches, why not ensure that coaches approach learning through an anti-racist lens, as well? For example, while a teacher may have great overall reading scores and feel confident in their instruction, maybe their ELL students are consistently struggling, or their few students of color in a predominantly white class are scoring lower than the rest. Perhaps, too, teachers aren't sure how to facilitate more conversation that interrogates and questions various perspectives in a text. Coaches are a great support to improve teacher confidence in approaching instruction through an anti-racist lens and, of course, increase student achievement. You can also connect teachers to people on the leadership team and others who are also growing as anti-racist educators. Having colleagues who are willing to share resources and discuss problems of practice is a valuable way for teachers to continue learning.

Step 4: Create spaces for more conversation.

Don't let professional development sessions be the only times teachers can discuss new learnings and ask questions. Create other ways for staff to work through questions and seek guidance. The process could look different in each school based on what the staff needs. One way to create this space is by forming a meeting structure for groups like a book club made up of teachers who are committed to anti-racist work and would like to have discussion groups. Also consider how to create virtual spaces such as a digital "parking lot" or discussion space for questions, topics, or situations that need follow-up or advice. These are good opportunities for staff to discuss challenges that come up for them both personally and in the classroom, as well as for sharing their learning, furthering their thinking, and asking questions.

Step 5: Provide meaningful feedback.

Specific and relevant feedback is necessary to improve practice. Providing feedback that directly addresses teacher practices and student performance is another way to support educators' growth as anti-racists. Both constructive and positive feedback help educators understand what authentic anti-racist instructional and environmental changes look like. One way for you to prepare to give feedback is to meet with teachers and learn their areas of confidence or struggle. These meetings can be powerful starting points because they will help you offer meaningful feedback that addresses a relevant need. Your feedback can address different challenges teachers face as they learn, including how to:

- utilize materials to introduce or interrogate different perspectives and information
- meet the needs of linguistically diverse learners
- address behaviors and build relationships with students
- facilitate conversations about sensitive or challenging topics
- incorporate relevant connections during lessons for students

- audit representation and messaging in the classroom environment and library

These are a few areas that may need support. Every educator is different, and it's valuable to give positive feedback so educators know what they are doing well and what they can build on. Feedback also boosts morale and trust.

BONUS NOTE

As teachers engage in a greater degree of conversations and learning, more questions and challenges are bound to arise, especially regarding student and staff situations, problematic thinking, and possible student resources. Intentionally empower teachers with resources, feedback, and chances to learn from one another. Such empowerment will support the endeavors of teachers of color and other individuals who have taken on leadership roles within equity work. While BIPOC individuals on anti-racism leadership teams may be expected to educate others within reason, adult learners are simultaneously encouraged to be self-directed in unpacking their own problematic beliefs and developing knowledge and understanding about racism and anti-racism.

At this point, it bears repeating that for Black, Indigenous, and other staff of color, the task of educating white people about race is often thrust upon us as a heavy emotional burden. Teachers of color are given the responsibility to address issues of racism and educate others about race-related issues. White people learning what it means to be anti-racist must also learn to speak out when they see issues of

> *racism, seek out their own learning, and be responsible for their own growth.*
>
> *Providing spaces and resources for teachers to engage in learning together and further their knowledge on their own is a meaningful action you can take to encourage authentic growth and empower adult learners.*

OVERCOMING PUSHBACK

Anti-racism is not a trend or buzzword, and you can help educators understand that, despite what opponents might say. The proof of why this work is necessary is all around us. We must be willing to look closely at the data, put pride to the side, listen to different perspectives, and be open to accepting (or at least considering) what might not be fully understood *yet*. The following are responses you might receive from those who are skeptical and how to answer them.

Anti-racism is just another politically correct trend that will come and go. Due to messaging from news outlets, politicians, and social media, some staff may feel that anti-racism is part of a trend or a larger nefarious agenda. So, we must lay the groundwork of providing supportive data, sharing student and staff experiences, and making clear connections to the history of race in America and within our communities. It's critical for staff to see that anti-racism goes beyond trends and agendas and is necessary for the growth and success of all students.

If this background information is not enough for teachers to be open to receiving support, take the time to get personal and build a relationship. Talk with and listen to teachers to understand what beliefs and histories drive their perspective. While there will always be people who disagree, getting personal when offering support helps move resistant staff from completely closing off to at least considering how this learning can benefit students.

I don't want to be judged. Often, people worry about saying the wrong thing or offending others when discussing race-related topics, so they avoid or opt out of the conversations altogether. While it is normal not to want to say something offensive, this is an example of using privilege to avoid discomfort. For BIPOC, we cannot opt out of racism, and often, we are expected to be okay with discussing race. The worry about being judged and the fear of being seen as racist can make people resistant to learning or accepting support outside of required professional development. They might even become defensive when faced with information about racism. For white people, this response is an example of white defensiveness, also known as white fragility, a term popularized by author Robin DiAngelo. The term refers to a range of negative responses such as anger, guilt, defensiveness, dismissiveness, and denial when faced with discussions about racism, race, discrimination, prejudice, or privilege.

Educators who aren't willing to grow or confront their racism shouldn't be teaching children, but the fact is that in many schools, they are. Because of this reality, trust needs to be developed between leaders and staff. While this is a long-term effort that requires great communication, transparency, and authentic relationship-building, developing a culture of trust helps staff to see that anti-racist leaders truly want what's best for students and are not "out to get" anyone. To move this work forward, teachers must be willing to be vulnerable and share stories and beliefs that shape who they are and how they think, accept feedback, and engage in learning that addresses areas where they need to grow. It's a tall order that is only met in environments where there is trust.

My students already perform well. Why do I need to change anything? Do test scores matter? Yes. But academic performance is not the only indicator of how teachers' biases affect students. Students are more than scores, and good educators know that teachers educate the whole child. They know that students bring with them their complete identities. While a student might not have the language or feel safe enough to tell their teacher when something that was said or done was racially insensitive or if they felt uncomfortable, that doesn't mean it never happens.

Students' social and emotional well-being is of primary importance. Consider this: Have students been encouraged to express how they feel and share their experiences? How can educators meet students' emotional needs if they don't see them holistically and work to ensure that they feel a sense of belonging? Developing a culture of growth and lifelong learning helps us improve our practices and gain a deeper understanding of our students' perspectives.

THE HACK IN ACTION

The following fictional story illustrates how to provide ongoing support. It was inspired by a variety of true events.

It was the end of another long day in Ms. Adams's fifth-grade classroom; she had just concluded a contentious phone call with a student's father. Today's conflict involved one of her students, Darrell, calling her racist because she asked him to stop tapping his pencil. Ms. Adams felt hurt, unnerved, and even a little angry by this accusation, so she called his father, Mr. Davis, yet again, to inform him about Darrell's disruptive behavior. These feelings were amplified when Mr. Davis replied, "Well, maybe you are," before conceding to speak with Darrell at home once again. Ms. Adams sent her principal a quick email to give a heads-up about the conversation.

Unfortunately, this was the second time she contacted Darrell's parents that week. A couple of days earlier, the principal, Ms. Clark, asked what Ms. Adams had done so far to build a stronger relationship with him and his parents. She thought that might help with the behavior issues, especially since Ms. Adams often sent Darrell to the office after what she felt were too many instances of disruption or disrespect. Darrell and another student were supposed to be working together on an assignment. But Ms. Adams heard them giggling, so she made Darrell work independently, and the other student, who was Latinx, partnered with someone else. Ms. Clark entered the room just as Darrell groaned that it wasn't fair that he had to work alone. Ms. Adams replied, "You're working alone because you keep distracting other classmates." Darrell started to retort, "That's not even what was happening!" However, Ms. Adams didn't want to hear any more about it and turned her attention back to the small group she was teaching. Darrell's accusations had gone from her not being fair to being racist, and now his father agreed. Ms. Adams wasn't sure how much more she could take if something didn't change.

That evening, the exchanges with Darrell and his dad played on a loop in Ms. Adams's mind. The more she thought about it, the more unsure she felt that she was completely in the right, which made her even more uncomfortable. Since the beginning of the year, she and Darrell had butted heads. He would often question her instructions and disrupt the class by talking to other students, making jokes, or making beats with the help of his pencil. Ms. Adams spoke to his father countless times and began thinking that he just didn't care enough to address his son's behavior, especially since Mr. Davis didn't sign up for parent conferences. Ms. Adams never once considered race a factor in the situation, and now he had called her a racist in front of the class. Sure, she was white, and he was Black, but that didn't mean she was automatically racist, right? Plus, the student that she allowed to continue working with a partner was Latinx. Ms. Adams had attended her school's professional development session on culturally responsive teaching, invested in stocking up her classroom library with diverse texts, and even joined the district's book club to read and discuss books on race. She thought to herself, *How could I be racist when I am willing to do all this learning and work in a school where the majority of students are BIPOC?* After thinking about the situation over and over and being unable to let it go, Ms. Adams decided to consult with a trusted colleague whom she'd gotten to know through the book club.

The next morning, before the bell rang to signal the start of the day, Ms. Adams stopped by Mrs. Richard's fourth-grade room. Mrs. Richard was a participant in the book club and led the anti-racist efforts on a committee at their school alongside a few other teachers. They happened to share the same preparation period, so Ms. Adams asked if they could meet soon to discuss the situation. When 2 p.m. rolled around, Ms. Adams made her way to Mrs. Richard's room. She was feeling a little anxious about sharing what Darrell had said. The last thing Ms. Adams wanted was for a student, or anyone, for that matter, to think that she was racist.

When she reached Mrs. Richard's room, they sat down, and Ms. Adams expressed how she had reached out to his parents many times, how his behavior continued to be disruptive, and that she was at the end of her patience when it came to trying to "reach" him, especially since he called her racist. To this, Mrs. Richard asked, "Have you asked him why he called you racist?"

Ms. Adams felt her cheeks heating up with embarrassment. Silence hung in the air. The answer was no. When he called her racist, she immediately replied that she wasn't, got defensive, and told him that what he said was hurtful. Ms. Adams hadn't thought to ask why at all. Mrs. Richard told her that this could have been, and still could be, the start of a valuable conversation. It was a chance for her to get to know Darrell and work toward repairing their relationship, as well as reflect on how her biases influenced the situation, as they had discussed in a professional learning session. Mrs. Richard also suggested that she look at the resource bank that had been shared by the anti-racism committee with suggestions for building relationships with parents, racial disparities in discipline, and white fragility.

Thanks to Mrs. Richard, Ms. Adams realized that up to this point, she had centered her own feelings and completely disregarded Darrell's perspective as a student in her class. Even though Ms. Adams was stressed out by what she deemed as disrespect and disruptiveness, she had failed to consider Darrell's sense of belonging or the validity of his experience. Walking back to her classroom, Ms. Adams resolved that she needed to be vulnerable and have a conversation with Darrell and that she would be dedicating time over the weekend to go through the resources Mrs. Richard had suggested.

On Monday, as she stood in the hallway, saying, "Good morning," Ms. Adams saw Darrell coming down the hall. Over the weekend, she had spent time browsing through the shared resources, reflecting on her actions, and considering her relationships with Darrell and his father. Ms. Adams acknowledged that even though she was willing to engage in learning about anti-racism, she needed to put into action what she had learned daily, not just when it was comfortable for her. The first action was to hold herself accountable for ignoring Darrell's feelings and to repair the relationship with his family. After her reading, she understood that her initial anger and defensiveness were a result of her own white fragility. Rather than attempting to understand where he was coming from, she had completely shut down the conversation out of fear and discomfort. Ms. Adams needed to be real about the fact that she had implicit racial biases, and they did affect her relationship with Darrell, whether or not it was intentional.

When all the students finally arrived, Ms. Adams walked over to Darrell as he hovered over his desk, unpacking his backpack and laughing with a friend. The smile he wore slowly faded as he saw her approaching. To his surprise, instead of asking him to quiet down or take a seat, she asked if they could talk privately once he settled in.

After Darrell set out his materials for the morning and Ms. Adams greeted the class and took attendance, Darrell followed her into the hallway to talk. It was uncommon for Ms. Adams to feel nervous or anticipate conversations with her students, but unlike other conversations, this one required a great deal of humility. "Darrell, I want to apologize to you," Ms. Adams said. Darrell's eyebrows knitted together in confusion, but he stayed silent. She went on, "Last week, I made an unfair decision to move you out of the pair you were in when you both were laughing. You told me I was being racist, and I am sorry for not listening to what you were feeling. We've had some challenging moments so far this year, but I want the rest of the year to be better. Even though I am an adult and a teacher, I also make mistakes. This is your classroom, too, and I want to make sure that I treat everyone who is a part of our classroom community fairly. So I think that during our morning meeting today, we should talk about the community agreements that we signed at the beginning of the school year. I think we could add something about fairness and talk about some examples of that in our classroom. What do you think?"

Darrell agreed. During the weeks after the conversation, whenever there was a moment when she would typically sternly address his behavior, she took a different approach. Ms. Adams started to privately check in with him, give him special tasks in the classroom, and take a moment (as much as possible) to reflect on whether or not she was reacting to his behavior in the same way as she would with other students in the class. It took time and patience for her to get used to this new approach, but through this simple change in her behavior management, she learned that the "disruptive behaviors" were often a result of Darrell finishing his work ahead of others, and when she took a moment to observe instead of react, she noted that other students were often engaged in the same behaviors.

Darrell was a bright student, and perhaps the problem wasn't Darrell being disruptive; perhaps it was that the work was not challenging him enough and her own misperceptions of behaviors in the classroom.

A couple of weeks later, Ms. Adams shared the situation with the book club after the prompt, "Does anyone want to share a problem of practice they faced this month?" After she had received sound advice from Mrs. Richard, Ms. Adams leaned into the idea of getting comfortable with being uncomfortable. Through the resources and talking with Darrell, she realized that just because she was "doing the work" didn't mean she wasn't going to make mistakes. More importantly, if she were committed to becoming anti-racist, she had to take responsibility when she messed up and learn from it.

Ms. Adams shared with the group what happened with Darrell and their conversation. The book club members probed further with the question, "Why didn't you notice this before?" The question was intriguing, and rather than giving an excuse, such as that she didn't have time to stop and check in constantly, or getting defensive, she was honest and admitted that after reading more about how bias and racism result in disproportionate disciplinary actions for Black boys, she needed to dig deeper and reflect on how this was playing out in her own classroom.

The day after the book club meeting, Ms. Adams was finishing up her whole-group math lesson when the principal came into her classroom for a brief walkthrough. The last time Ms. Clark visited her classroom, she had witnessed an unproductive exchange between Ms. Adams and Darrell. This time, the energy in the classroom was much different. Ms. Clark watched how Ms. Adams checked in with Darrell as he shut his notebook and turned to talk with a neighbor. As Ms. Clark left the room, she slipped a note onto Ms. Adams's desk. It read, "I noticed how you quietly checked in with Darrell and redirected him. It seems like you're starting to build a positive relationship. I think his parents would love to hear this!" Connecting with Darrell's parents was the one task Ms. Adams had avoided. She knew she had to reach out and work on mending the relationship, especially after the pivotal conversation with Darrell a couple of weeks ago, but it felt like a daunting task. Nonetheless, she resolved to call his father after school. Ms. Adams wanted to be the best teacher she could be for her students and recognized the importance of developing a positive relationship with parents as well as hearing their perspectives. One conversation wouldn't fix the damage that had been done, but it would be a step in the right direction.

As teachers learn about anti-racism, ongoing support and access to resources are crucial to continue building on knowledge and, most importantly, applying what they've learned. As new situations come up, educators need spaces to work through problems together so they can improve their practice and truly understand what anti-racism looks like in the classroom. Providing a support system through colleagues, readily available relevant materials, and specific feedback helps you to encourage the growth of educators as they meet the challenges that come with developing an anti-racist lens. As we learn more, we can do better, and receiving ongoing support allows educators to develop better practices to meet the needs of all students.

HACK 5

INTENTIONALLY SUPPORT BIPOC EDUCATORS
RECRUIT AND RETAIN WITH PURPOSE

> *We will all, at some point, encounter hurdles to gaining access and entry, moving up and conquering self-doubt, but on the other side is the capacity to own opportunity and tell our own story.*
> – STACEY ABRAMS, POLITICIAN, LAWYER, AND ACTIVIST

THE PROBLEM: SCHOOLS HAVE DIFFICULTY RECRUITING AND RETAINING BIPOC EDUCATORS

IN THE 2017–2018 school year, the National Center for Education Statistics (NCES) reported that public school teachers of color accounted for 20 percent of all teachers, while students of color made up 52 percent. These numbers highlight the lack of representation of BIPOC teachers in the workforce. Many school districts struggle to recruit teachers of color and have difficulty maintaining environments where they feel supported and valued enough to stay. Just as Black, Indigenous, and other students of color face racism, bias, and discrimination in schools, BIPOC working in school settings experience this as well, and often, little, if anything, is done to support those dealing with these emotionally draining interactions.

In addition to this, educators of color carry the burden of what has been deemed the "invisible tax," which former Secretary of Education Dr. John King discusses in an opinion piece in *The Washington Post* as "the invisible tax on teachers of color." It means the emotional toll that Black, Indigenous, and other educators of color experience when we must navigate racism, are expected to take on the responsibilities of all things related to race and diversity, and are seen as representatives of cultural diversity and BIPOC perspectives. An increased burden, coupled with a lack of support, often leads to immense stress and burnout for educators. While we, BIPOC educators, have long dealt with and found ways to survive these challenges, it has been at a great cost. Schools and districts need to do more to acknowledge and eliminate these stressors.

THE HACK: INTENTIONALLY SUPPORT BIPOC EDUCATORS

Being an educator, no matter the role, is difficult. Being an educator of color and facing the common occurrences of microaggressions, macroaggressions, and other racist encounters adds another layer of emotional and potentially physical distress. By deciding to teach and learn through a lens of anti-racism, schools can begin to put systems and structures in place that will support staff when they face incidents of racism and that will promote a culture where racism is not tolerated. Providing intentional support that considers the specific experiences of BIPOC educators creates an environment where teachers can thrive and are encouraged to come to work as their whole selves. Not only does this make for a healthier, more encouraging work environment for adults, but it also creates a more positive climate for students.

Being a BIPOC educator in a school with predominantly white staff can feel extremely isolating, even if we have positive, supportive working relationships with white colleagues. Even in schools with diverse teacher populations, educators still endure racism, as well as carry internalized racist ideologies. When incidents involving race occur, teachers and administrators may not know who to turn to for advice or an empathetic ear, especially because colleagues might not understand the situation or may invalidate their perspectives. By providing intentional support, your school can acknowledge experiences that are specific to BIPOC educators and proactively create environments where they feel seen, heard, and valued.

Hack 5 includes ways to share and create opportunities for connection with other educators. As mentioned, having trusted people to go to for guidance and support is powerful and helps us grow; for BIPOC educators, it can also be critical to our resilience and preservation. Offering these connections creates spaces where educators feel affirmed and understood. Another way this Hack may take shape within your school is in how ideas and interactions regarding race are recognized and acknowledged. Are BIPOC experiences centered during professional learning? Are people comfortable discussing the realities of racism and injustice within our society and school? Do educators call out racism when they see it, whether in an interaction or data? Providing intentional support to BIPOC educators will require you to take an honest look at the culture and climate around race within your school and consider what needs to be done.

Another crucial piece of providing intentional support to BIPOC educators is to foster an environment where racism is not tolerated. So often, schools and districts tout statements, webpages, and initiatives supporting anti-racism and all the ways they are working to decrease racial inequities. At the same time, they are not always taking action when situations arise or attention is called to specific issues. Such situations might take the form of racist jokes and comments being "brushed off," individuals not being held accountable for racist behavior, a lack of clear pathways or structures for addressing racism in the workplace, no attention given to racial inequities in academic or behavior data beyond merely noticing it, BIPOC educators being the *only* ones expected to initiate or continue anti-racist work, and anti-racism professional learning without accountability. These are a handful of ways that schools and districts frequently fail to authentically create environments where anti-racism is more than a new topic for the year.

In any educational environment, providing intentional support for educators of color encourages continued growth as professionals within the field, as well as positive mental health and well-being. The support provided will look different depending on the needs of the individuals you work with, the culture and climate of the school, and the historical and present-day impact of race relations within your school and community. Without intentionality, informed planning, and thoughtful execution, efforts can come across as performative and inefficacious. It is critical to understand how race and racism shape the lives of BIPOC individuals so we can offer support that sincerely addresses the challenges we face.

Intentionally Support BIPOC Educators

WHAT YOU CAN DO TOMORROW

Disrupting the status quo will always come with challenges. Even though supporting initiatives that change our norms takes time to implement and see the results, we have to be willing to start somewhere. Once an inequity has been acknowledged, we cannot be afraid of "rocking the boat" to move forward. The following short-term tasks offer ways for your school to establish or bolster support for educators of color.

- **Find out what relevant data is available.** As with any new step, analyzing relevant data helps to strengthen and defend your next move. Staff demographic data that is disaggregated by race creates a more accurate and informed picture of the employee population. You can also organize this data by certified and non-certified staff and years of service. Looking for patterns and trends develops a stronger understanding of the past and present, as well as highlights any significant changes. In addition to demographic data, does your school or district conduct staff surveys on climate or culture? Depending on the survey questions, this anecdotal data can be helpful to gain a deeper understanding of the experiences of BIPOC educators within the school as well as the general views and beliefs of the staff. As you analyze data, here are some questions to prompt your thinking:

- Are there years with a more or less diverse teacher population? Why might this be? Were there policies, leadership changes, hiring practices, partnerships with local teacher prep programs, or any other factors that would have informed the numbers at the time?
  - What is the comparison of certified and non-certified staff of color?
  - What is the representation of BIPOC administrators?
  - Are there BIPOC teachers or other staff who have worked at the school or in the district for a long time (for example, more than ten years)? How can you learn about their experiences?
  - How many early career teachers of color are there? What attracted them to your school or district? How can you learn about what they need to stay and be successful?
- **Learn about the historical backdrop of racial history in the community.** The past informs the present. As you investigate historical data on teacher demographics of the school, you can also frame this information within the historical context of the community where you work. Reach out and talk to community members.
  - What have been the attitudes and beliefs about race and racial relations? Has the

racial demographic of the population changed? If so, how has the community responded?
- Do elected leaders within the community reflect the demographics of the community?
- What is the history of segregation and integration within the community?
- What happened to Black teachers in your area after legal segregation ended?
- If you are in an independent school, what is the school's history with racial relations?

These questions will help you gain more context about the data regarding the teacher population. Moreover, understanding local history helps inform the attitudes and beliefs that BIPOC educators might face from families, colleagues, and other members of the community.

- **Talk with the staff.** Talking with educators within your school or district is key. Instead of making decisions based on assumptions about what BIPOC educators experience or what white educators believe about race, make time to connect and listen. Listen with the intention of learning, without jumping in to suggest a solution or holding an attitude of disbelief. In many of my interactions when talking with white people about racism, my descriptions have often been met with some form of disbelief, excuse, or sympathy for the perpetrator because "maybe they didn't mean it like

that," or "they're just ignorant." If you are seeking to create an anti-racist culture and environment, you must believe BIPOC when they share their stories, and you must hold people accountable—not dismissing racism and excusing behavior.
- **Discover what funds are available.** Begin looking into funds awarded or granted by organizations supporting racial equity, educators, or professional development. Many organizations support the diversification of the education profession by offering opportunities to receive funding. Additionally, connect with school and district administrators to inquire about pathways to putting funding toward supporting the recruitment and retention of BIPOC educators.

A BLUEPRINT FOR FULL IMPLEMENTATION

Step 1: Use the data to inform your first move.

Data tells a story. What story do you learn from teacher demographic and retention data and how can you make this data work for you? Just as student achievement data tells educators what areas need improvement, data about teachers informs you about where to begin efforts. For example, if you found that early-career teachers of color were not staying long, consider starting with creating options for mentorship, which we'll discuss next. If you have few BIPOC educators in your school or district, you may want to start with a focus on recruitment; however, consider whether recruitment efforts will be effective if educators are coming into problematic, harmful environments. Recruitment is part of increasing teacher diversity, but it's not the only route. First, or concurrently, put systems into place that support prospective and current BIPOC teachers.

Step 2: Offer opportunities for mentorship and connection.

Mentorship is a powerful tool for educators at all career levels. For early-career educators, mentorship has the potential to develop their instructional practices, behavior management, ability to work through problems of practice, and coping skills with the emotional challenges of being a new educator. For BIPOC educators at all career levels, having a mentor or other educators of color to learn from and connect with also provides opportunities to work through experiences specific to our identities, whether situations concern students, families, or staff. Discussing racial dilemmas with people who share them can lessen feelings of isolation. Perhaps your school or district can create structures to connect BIPOC educators as mentors and mentees. You can also create an affinity group for staff of color. Racial affinity groups offer safe spaces for educators to connect with those who share experiences and challenges unique to their racial identity. These connections help foster a stronger sense of belonging and affirmation and a space to feel seen and heard after emotional or traumatic racial offenses. These are also spaces where educators continue to grow in their professional capacity as teachers and leaders.

Step 3: Present opportunities for professional growth and leadership development.

What options can educators find for out-of-district professional learning? These options are especially useful if you cannot yet facilitate professional learning that is aligned with anti-racist values or inclusive of the viewpoints of educators of color. Encourage BIPOC educators to seek this learning elsewhere. Speakers, conferences, workshops, and professional network memberships are all great ways to support your educators in finding community and developing their professional skills. Yes, this type of support requires a financial commitment, but an investment in educators is an investment in students. Supporting educators to continue evolving their professional skills helps them to be better prepared for the challenges they'll face in their roles. As a result, this supports retention efforts and preparation for leadership roles in the future.

Step 4: Promote leadership development.

Do school and district leaders represent the student population? Is it diverse? How many BIPOC educators hold leadership roles? If leadership is also predominantly white, consider creating a pipeline to leadership and developing the capacity of teachers to become teacher leaders and, eventually, school and district leaders. Educators can serve in official leadership roles on committees and teams that oversee school and district initiatives within and outside of racial equity efforts. Do not limit BIPOC educators to explicit equity and anti-racist work. Give educators paid opportunities to share knowledge with others by planning and facilitating professional development and working directly with current school and district leadership to analyze data and roll out or pilot schoolwide initiatives.

As educators develop their knowledge and skills to become strong instructional leaders, your school or district could consider ways to support them in obtaining advanced certification and degrees for leadership positions. Support could include tuition reimbursement, leader mentorship, or some form of a pipeline for them to eventually work within the school or district in an official leadership capacity. Creating pathways for BIPOC teachers to become leaders supports retention and recruitment efforts to diversify school- and district-level leadership. It also helps build community and connection for leaders of color and lessen feelings of isolation in leadership roles such as principalship, which can typically feel lonely, even without disparities in race.

Step 5: Create systems for accountability.

One way to weave the importance of equity into the fabric of school communities is by creating systems for accountability. Not only is this a significant way to measure implementation and effectiveness, but it also offers pathways for BIPOC staff to seek support when facing a dilemma. Many times, staff of color endure racial offenses and prejudices directed at them or students. How they handle these moments is critical. Is there a trusted person they can process with? Is there a reporting system that results in learning and accountability? So often, Black, Indigenous, and other people of color are left to figure out how to handle the situation on their own, or the issues go unaddressed for a myriad of reasons. Whether or not the offense was committed with innocent or malicious intentions does not matter. The harm has been done, and if not repaired, it contributes to the factors that push Black and Brown educators out of the profession. If BIPOC educators within your school report a problematic, racist offense, how is it handled? What conversations, learnings, and, if necessary, consequences take place afterward? Does school leadership know how to handle these situations confidently? Administrators must also engage in learning about anti-racism so they can productively address incidents of racism and gain staff trust in their leadership to do so.

> **CREATING PATHWAYS FOR BIPOC TEACHERS TO BECOME LEADERS IN AN OFFICIAL CAPACITY SUPPORTS RETENTION AND RECRUITMENT EFFORTS TO DIVERSIFY SCHOOL- AND DISTRICT-LEVEL LEADERSHIP.**

Another form of accountability is to clearly and explicitly thread the connections and expectations of anti-racist teaching and learning into observations, goal-setting, and feedback.

Unfortunately, observation processes often serve more as a dreaded compliance measure than valued learning. These experiences can be ways to receive honest, meaningful feedback that grows an individual professionally and possibly personally. If we treat observations as meaningful opportunities for growth and not as "gotcha" moments, they can help school leaders see how to implement anti-racist practices authentically in classrooms and provide teachers with useful feedback to evolve their practice in ways that promote equity and inclusion. To incorporate anti-racism or CRSP meaningfully into the observation process, the onus is on the administration to develop trust with staff members and create a culture of continuous growth and feedback. For example, giving teachers voice and choice in their growth goals, regularly offering positive and thoughtful feedback, and providing resources and learning for growth are three ways to develop more positive engagement around the evaluation process.

As mentioned in earlier chapters, when there are few BIPOC educators in a school, they may be seen as the go-to resource for all things related to race and culture. While they may well be a great source of knowledge, it is another example of the "invisible tax," which becomes wearisome. Utilizing already-present methods of feedback, such as the observation process, continues to develop anti-racist teaching and learning practices and lessens the unsolicited expectation of BIPOC educators to be a constant resource.

Step 6: Recruit more educators of color.

Recruiting more BIPOC educators is purposefully left for last because, as critical as it is to increase the diversity of staff in schools, we must first strive to create safe environments where educators of color will be supported and want to stay. Let's not recruit new BIPOC educators only to throw them into detrimental environments where they will quickly burn out. However, if you are making improvements to be more inclusive and responsive to the needs of educators of color, moving forward with recruitment is a significant step. Schools can pursue recruitment efforts in many ways. The best strategies for your district will vary depending on available resources and where you are located. Here are five strategies to recruit more educators of color.

1. **Create a pipeline for students within the district to pursue careers in education.** Many school districts have some variation of "future educator" clubs. In these clubs, students of color can be given chances to visit local colleges, build mentor-mentee relationships with current educators in the district, and hear from panels of educators of color. They also can receive guidance in college financial planning, financial aid application support, and scholarship applications. You can find other creative ways to envision supporting students based on the needs of your population.

2. **Connect with teacher preparation programs.** Prep programs offer an effective way to begin building relationships with college advisors and pre-service teachers of color. Student teachers will sometimes apply for a job in the district where they interned. Even if you are not a partner district for student teaching, you can still build relationships with post-secondary schools so that advisors are aware of openings within your district. It's also beneficial to participate in their career fairs. These relationships can also result in opportunities for current secondary students of color to visit the campus and learn about teacher preparation programs. Also, seek

out relationships with historically Black colleges and universities (HBCUs) and colleges with greater populations of BIPOC students. Even on predominantly white campuses, you can reach out to student groups that serve students of color. Making these connections and getting the word out about your school or district is a good way to bring in new teachers of color as they apply for jobs.

3. **Hire early.** I can exemplify this best through my personal experience. As I was starting to look for teaching jobs, a wonderful friend, Orlando (you'll learn more about him later), told me that I should apply to the district he was teaching in. I applied, was interviewed, and accepted a position before even crossing the graduation stage that spring. It was my first and only interview. Had the district not moved quickly, I would have continued seeking out other districts. My story is similar to the stories of multiple BIPOC educators I know. Create a timeline to seek out BIPOC candidates, and hire them early!

4. **Ensure a diverse hiring committee.** Even if your school or district is mostly white, strive to make the hiring committee as diverse as possible for all applicants. Having a diverse representation of committee members is not about making it seem like your school community is more diverse than it is, but this offers various perspectives of the candidate, uplifts the voices of different members of the school community, offers an introduction to organizational values and culture, and potentially makes the applicant feel more comfortable, which gives a

Intentionally Support BIPOC Educators

more authentic view of who they are and if they're a good candidate for the position. All individuals, no matter their background, hold implicit bias. Those who partake in any part of the hiring process must engage in anti-bias training to provide a more fair and equitable hiring process and recognize desirable candidates who might otherwise be passed over. In addition to having a diverse hiring committee and anti-bias training, look closely at the questions asked during interviews. How do they give the committee a glimpse into the deeply held beliefs of the interviewee, and do these beliefs align with the school culture and anti-racist values? One way to do this is to present scenarios incorporating diversity, equity, inclusion, or belonging. These scenarios are reflective of the position the candidates are applying for and a situation that is realistic to the school climate and culture. Here is an example of a scenario:

- Scenario: A Black student in your class expresses to you that they think another student, who is white, is racist after they've continuously called them the name of another Black student in the class. How would you handle this situation?

Separately, you might ask:

- What education around DEI have you participated in, and how has it impacted your role as an educator? If you haven't had any, what is your understanding of DEI in a school environment?

These types of questions or scenarios offer the participants an opportunity to respond in a way that demonstrates their level of comfort, knowledge, or willingness to grow regarding diversity, equity, and inclusion (DEI) and related topics. It's necessary to determine what you're looking for. Are you seeking individuals who have a strong understanding of DEI and its importance, or are you willing to accept an individual who has a basic, if any, understanding but is willing to grow? Importantly, will your school be prepared to support them in that growth? Just as we want to avoid recruiting BIPOC into harmful environments, we also want to avoid hiring individuals who aren't willing to grow as anti-racist educators.

5. **Provide support for certification and credentialing.** In many states, the requirements for certification ask potential educators to overcome great hurdles. Whether highly desired candidates are navigating a complicated application system or the steep financial cost of certification, districts can offer support to those who would otherwise meet the position's needs. This support could include guidance in navigating application processes, financial assistance, recommendations of alternative certification programs, and other unique methods based on the barriers candidates are facing. If your school has power over the qualifications required for a position, carefully consider what you are looking for and what candidates need to succeed.

OVERCOMING PUSHBACK

This Hack—particularly about intentionally hiring BIPOC educators—can be difficult for individuals to understand. However, white students benefit from having diverse racial representation among their teachers, and research presented in "The Added Value of Latinx and Black Teachers for Latinx and Black Students" by Travis J. Bristol and Javier Martin-Fernandez makes it clear that BIPOC students benefit from having BIPOC teachers. Not only is this diversity good for students, but we should want our school staff to reflect the diverse world we live in. With diversity comes diverse perspectives, strengths, new ideas, and new ways of doing things. While the intentional support of BIPOC educators may cause some to give pushback, this act of resistance to the effects of racism and discrimination is more than worth the benefits to students and society at large. Here are a few common concerns and how to address them.

It's not fair to give support and opportunities based on race. The belief that offering more support to underprivileged groups is unfair is typically rooted in the fear of losing privilege. To address issues stemming from systemic racism, such as low recruitment and retention of BIPOC educators, we need solutions that tackle the core of the problem. For example, if we know feelings of isolation cause teachers to leave, let's create opportunities for connection. If fewer BIPOC educators are moving into leadership roles because they do not have the necessary credentials or degrees, build capacity for leadership through professional development and support their progress toward needed certification. Also, consider the "qualifications" and if they are truly necessary for success in the role. If qualified BIPOC candidates are being passed over for leadership roles, then this requires analyzing the promotion or hiring process to figure out where bias and racism influence these decisions.

> WITH DIVERSITY COMES DIVERSE PERSPECTIVES, STRENGTHS, NEW IDEAS, AND NEW WAYS OF DOING THINGS.

Anti-Racist Teaching

Every person deserves an equal playing field to achieve success. Data on racial disparities in education (and in many other aspects of society) shows that this still has not been achieved due to a deep history of unequal access to resources and opportunities because of racism. To address this, we must apply solutions within our sphere of influence that level the playing field and offer opportunities to individuals who have been historically excluded and marginalized.

We don't need to have a system for reporting racial incidents; people are too sensitive. Students are encouraged to have empathy and use appropriate language when communicating, and educators are expected to be role models for this in the workplace. If an individual does not understand why a word, phrase, joke, or comment is inappropriate or offensive, then have a process or pathway for learning why. No one wants or deserves to be on the receiving end of racist offenses in their workplace and then be expected to teach the individual why what they said or did was harmful.

Additionally, as times change, so does language and what is deemed acceptable and appropriate. Schools can help the community to be aware of changes in language, and it is our professional responsibility to accept and practice these changes. For example, if a colleague is still using the word "colored" for Black people, we can provide education on current terms and more specific language when referencing various racial and ethnic communities. By having a system for individuals to ask for support in these situations, school leaders can be made aware of what learning they need to offer to address the situation and communicate with individuals who require more direct accountability for offensive behavior. It is not an issue of "sensitivity" to expect colleagues to use appropriate language in the workplace. Professionals are expected to act as such, including treating each other with respect for one another's identities.

A teacher's race doesn't matter. How does this help students? Studies show the benefits of students having teachers of color include higher expectations for Black students and a lesser likelihood that negative biases will affect the teacher's perspectives of students of color. A research brief by Desiree Carver-Thomas, "Diversifying the Teaching Profession Through High-Retention Pathways," shows that benefits also include:

- increasing the academic performance of students of color through improved math and reading test scores, graduation rates, and students' desires to attend college
- decreasing the likelihood of chronic absenteeism and suspension (a social-emotional benefit, too)
- helping students feel cared for and academically challenged

These benefits show that diversifying the teacher workforce is a commitment to support teachers, lessen feelings of isolation, and create a greater positive impact on our students. An investment in teachers is an investment in our students, and by providing intentional support to hire and retain educators of color, we are also supporting students' academic success.

THE HACK IN ACTION

Unlike the previous Hack in Action sections, this one is a collection of narratives that demonstrate the experiences of three BIPOC educators. As you will see throughout these narratives, our journeys have many ups and downs, trials, and successes. Two themes are how school leadership is essential in creating opportunities where educators' gifts can shine, and how we, BIPOC educators, can champion each other.

In 1998, Lysette Torres stepped into a classroom to begin her career in education as a sixth-grade English teacher in her hometown in Connecticut. Lysette was born and raised in what was once known as the "Silver City" and attended the city's public schools, where she would later teach. Since then, Dr. Torres has earned her doctorate and served as an assistant principal, principal, and director of equity and instruction for the city's public schools. *As a Latina and first-generation college graduate, her journey was shaped by her identity, which led her to serve in roles that would propel efforts to support and recruit teachers of color.*

Often, Lysette would sit in the back corner of her high school honors classes, feeling invisible among her majority white classmates. As a student, Lysette was one of a much smaller number of students of color, whereas today, well over half of the students attending her public school district are students of color. Although she was a high-achieving student, Lysette felt unseen and was even told she "didn't belong" in her honors English class by the teacher, even though her grades and achievements said otherwise.

Lysette wanted to become a mentor for students like herself, so she returned to the Silver City as a middle school English teacher. Some years later, she would begin teaching at the same high school she once attended. As the only teacher of color in her department, Lysette was told that they "didn't need someone who was Spanish in the English department." Instead of allowing this to set her back, Lysette continued to show up for the students and worked even harder to ensure there were never issues with her work or performance.

She connected with the principal of the high school, who was also Puerto Rican, who shared some of the challenges she faced on the journey of earning her doctorate. This inspired Lysette to pursue her doctorate in education. She conducted research to study the "Determinants of Job Satisfaction and Dissatisfaction of Hispanic Principals in Connecticut." At the time (2000–2005), the pool of Hispanic administrators in Connecticut was under twenty-five. When Lysette moved from teaching to administration, the reality of the low numbers of Hispanic administrators was evident, although she did find community within the district.

A fellow administrator who was also Hispanic made it a point to take Lysette under his wing and support her from the moment he sat on her interview committee to the present day. Later, he would be a part of the equity efforts Lysette would lead.

In 2020, the district chose Dr. Torres, who was serving as an elementary principal at the time, for the director of equity and instruction role, which she welcomed. Having been a student, teacher, and building administrator, Dr. Torres had a longevity lens of what students and staff experienced and areas for improvement. While she did have positive examples, the microaggressions and macroaggressions she faced, as well as the lack of change since she was a student, indicated that there hadn't been enough progress. As the first person in this new role, she did harbor some feelings of fear, but Dr. Torres also recognized that she could connect with other BIPOC educators who had also been engaging in racial equity work. One of these educators was Orlando Valentin.

Orlando Valentin graduated from a technical high school in his hometown, also the Silver City, in 2011. Although he completed high school as a straight-A student and even a salutatorian, the start of his collegiate journey was a challenge. However, with the support and encouragement of other educators, Orlando began serving as an educator in his hometown's public school district in 2016 as a fourth-grade teacher, then later became an assistant principal after completing the administrator preparation program at his collegiate alma mater.

"Kids from tech schools don't typically make it in these programs" was the guidance an advisor gave to Orlando, who had just graduated from a technical high school and joined the engineering program at his university. Orlando had gone from excelling throughout his K–12 education to struggling in the engineering program, facing discouragement, and not feeling connected to his coursework. Thankfully, educators in his circle offered guidance, including two aunts working as teachers and Dr. Miguel Cardona, appointed Secretary of Education in 2021. These individuals offered the guidance that led Orlando to pursue a degree in teaching.

Orlando began his career in education as a fourth-grade teacher in his hometown. While classroom management can often be a challenge for new educators, this was Orlando's strength. He had a strong rapport with students, families, and the community through activities such as teaching martial arts and coaching football. He also ran a "diplomatic classroom"—students always had a voice and choice. He made it a point to treat students with the utmost respect and celebrate them. In turn, they performed at a high level. Academically, Orlando was offered the support of instructional coaching to continue growing as an educator and improving his practice. His growth also drew the attention of his administrators. As early as his second year of teaching, Orlando was appointed as the data team leader for his grade level—a role that increased his organizational and facilitation skills.

His journey, however, came with challenges. At times, he would notice microaggressions in the words colleagues were saying to and about students and recognized his own need to grow in confidence to speak up and call out these moments. It's a common challenge, especially as one of a few, or the only, BIPOC teachers in the building—as Orlando was for some time—and he was still gaining confidence as an educator. Nevertheless, Orlando did find his voice to call out these incidents, share his opinion, and ask a simple yet powerful question when needed: "What do you mean by that?" to encourage colleagues to reflect and feel the discomfort of their words.

As Orlando continued to develop his expertise and convictions, he was supported in furthering his growth as a budding leader.

Louis, a district administrator, was instrumental in Orlando's leadership journey. When the district's Leadership Academy was accepting applications, Louis reached out directly to Orlando and encouraged him to apply for this great chance to develop as a leader. In this academy, Orlando engaged in activities to learn about leadership pedagogy, discussion groups, and a project to implement change within his building. Louis also shared information with Orlando about a consortium for connecting teachers of color in Connecticut. Orlando followed up on opportunities to attend events, which he did faithfully every month for two years. There, he networked and made connections with many other accomplished individuals working in various roles in education throughout the state. Such collaborations led to the creation of an affinity group for BIPOC employees within the school district, as well as securing grant funds for scholarships and buying diverse children's and professional learning books to start "Equity Libraries" in every school.

Throughout this time, Orlando had a growing passion for recruiting BIPOC educators. As mentioned, I am a product of Orlando's recruitment efforts. Whenever a person of color entered the school, he made it a point to introduce himself and connect. Jason Hayes, a tutor at the time, was another one of the connections Orlando made.

Orlando met Jason Hayes when Jason was hired as a tutor at the school where Orlando taught. As the relationship progressed, not only did they become friends, but Jason also helped Orlando review and write grants. Orlando was Jason's advisor, and Jason eventually became the first resident of a certain alternative certification program in the district and student-taught in Orlando's classroom. Jason is now a specialist teacher, but unlike Lysette and Orlando, educating in a K–12 setting was not what he anticipated until his skills and the support he received determined otherwise.

Jason understood the difficulties that school often presented to students, especially as someone who dealt with the challenges of dyslexia. This exceptionality, coupled with the fact that some of his primary teachers were unprepared to meet his needs, often left Jason feeling frustrated and unheard.

His mother, who was an educator, advocated for him and entered Jason into an after-school program where he got the extra support he needed to eventually graduate and be accepted at a university. But again, he struggled. His mother encouraged him to take art courses to improve his grade point average. Her encouragement led to a fateful decision that resulted in Jason earning a degree in art. Later, after moving to Connecticut, he earned his master's degree in nonprofit work.

Years later, after trying out different jobs in the nonprofit world that were not a good fit or that treated him poorly, his wife suggested he apply for a job in the same school where Orlando was teaching. While Jason intended to become a Climate Specialist, the school's principal instead made him a tutor. In this role, he taught kids to read and supported their academic success, which felt like a great change. The principal also saw Jason's positive connection with the students. Both the principal and Orlando tried to persuade Jason to teach, encouraging him to talk with Louis to learn more about pathways to teacher certification. Eventually, Jason became an English for Speakers of Other Languages (ESOL) tutor, partnering with the head teacher in the ESOL program. Here, his gifts shined even more. Having had his own tumultuous experience as a student, he empathized with the kids he worked with and wanted to excel in this role to identify their areas of need and support them.

Eventually, with the encouragement of people like Orlando, Louis, and his principal, Mr. C, Jason enrolled in and completed an alternative teacher certification program. Mr. C allowed him to complete his student teaching with Orlando while continuing his work as a tutor. After completing the program, Louis offered Jason a position as an art teacher. While Jason's art skills were out of practice since earning his degree over twenty years earlier, engaging with youth in his class felt like second nature. He focused on supporting students and creating an environment where they were both motivated to be successful in class and challenged to be their best selves in all spaces of the school, regardless of who was teaching them. Jason felt the importance of his role as an educator and as a Black male teacher, and he facilitated dialogue with students about the value of who they are and the realities of the world they live in. Becoming an art teacher years after taking art courses to improve his GPA was a fortuitous circumstance of fate for both him and the students he serves.

"It's been more fun than I thought it would be," Jason said. Teaching was not what Jason planned on doing, but the career seemed to find him. Jason moved to Connecticut after working for years in various programs in different states. These roles included positions at nonprofits, working to support students who were struggling in school, serving in after-school programs, and substitute teaching. Throughout all these activities, Jason was fueled by the desire to help students be successful.

Understanding the challenges that many BIPOC educators face and making systemic changes to address them is fundamental to being an institution that truly values the diversity and well-being of educators. Throughout the stories of Lysette, Orlando, and Jason, each had difficulties in their journey toward becoming educators in the roles they are in now, and they had individuals who disrupted barriers and offered support. Imagine the world of education if this targeted, individualistic support were standard. These actions foster environments where BIPOC educators can thrive in the classroom and grow in their leadership, which, in turn, positively impacts the recruiting and retaining of BIPOC educators. Racism and prejudice continue to adversely affect the retention and recruitment of BIPOC educators, so our efforts must be intentional to promote both the skill development and holistic welfare of educators.

HACK 6

GET STUDENTS ENGAGED
CREATE OPPORTUNITIES FOR STUDENTS TO BE ACTIVELY INVOLVED

We have a powerful potential in our youth, and we must have the courage to change old ideas and practices so that we may direct their power toward good ends.
– MARY MCLEOD BETHUNE, EDUCATOR, ACTIVIST, AND PHILANTHROPIST

THE PROBLEM: STUDENTS NEED TO BE DIRECTLY INVOLVED IN DEI WORK

PROVIDING STAFF WITH opportunities to learn about anti-racism and supporting their application of this learning is a necessary precursor to engaging students in these conversations. As staff apply what they've learned, they may be unsure about how to directly engage students in this work, outside of teaching lessons. Hack 6 offers ideas about engaging students in conversations around diversity, equity, and inclusion so they are involved in meaningful and developmentally appropriate ways. Students can provide firsthand insight into what they are experiencing at school and what needs to be improved, and they have the agency to be changemakers.

Directly engaging students also helps to address the misconception that an anti-racist, culturally responsive, and sustaining environment means finding all new materials and lessons. While the work will influence the curriculum and instruction, students can be at the center in many other ways. As you implement changes that influence the school's climate, culture, and practices, be conscientious about how you promote adult growth in tandem with how you develop direct support for students. While educators' knowledge and understanding grow, we must communicate the importance of connecting this learning to student engagement and growth and consider how students are empowered as a result. With intentional efforts, the application of new learning will meaningfully impact students and create valuable experiences.

THE HACK: GET STUDENTS ENGAGED

As your school engages in professional learning to support anti-racism, you'll want to be intentional about how you involve students. Create ways for students to participate in anti-racist efforts that go beyond adding books and creating diverse libraries. Although these elements are extremely valued, students need opportunities to actively engage in discourse with each other and with high-quality resources.

By involving students in anti-racist learning, you create an environment that values and affirms their identities and amplifies their voices. For many students, school is where they learn—usually inferentially or unintentionally—what cultural identities and behaviors are most valued and considered the "norm." Through anti-racist learning, students are supported in developing their own positive identities and learning about identities different from their own.

Additionally, anti-racist teaching and learning requires students to think critically and engage in discourse designed to strengthen their independent thinking and reasoning. Not only is this a necessary life skill, but it also supports their academic growth and development as members of society. Anti-racist teaching will provide opportunities for students to learn about various topics that broaden their worldview and help them understand experiences that shaped who they are, as well as develop empathy for those with different life experiences.

> **FOR MANY STUDENTS, SCHOOL IS A PLACE WHERE THEY LEARN—USUALLY INFERENTIALLY OR UNINTENTIONALLY— WHAT CULTURAL IDENTITIES AND BEHAVIORS ARE MOST VALUED AND CONSIDERED THE "NORM."**

Beyond the academic benefits, engaging students directly develops a stronger sense of belonging and school community. Schools can be places where students do not feel valued, particularly students of color in settings that lack racial diversity. By creating an environment that celebrates the identities that make up a school and community, educators nurture a stronger sense of belonging and support the connectedness of the school community. This practice is also beneficial for predominantly white schools and communities. Students need to understand that there is no cultural identity that is the "norm" and that all individuals have culture. Working to develop a sense of belonging and school community will help students build deeper connections with one another and gain a better understanding of their own diverse identities.

Getting students engaged in anti-racist learning looks different across many environments, depending on your school's needs and capabilities. Ranging from lesson content and instruction, student-run and student-centered activities, to providing opportunities to hear about student experiences, many ways exist to ensure that anti-racist efforts are directly benefiting students. Making an intentional effort to impact students will also help educators to continually evolve their practice while directly supporting students' academic growth and social-emotional skills. No matter your school makeup, this Hack will benefit all students.

WHAT YOU CAN DO TOMORROW

As you provide ongoing support to educators, you can determine what students and the school community truly need. As with any change, you'll want to ensure it meets your students' needs while also nurturing a culture where the efforts will be sustained and championed. Therefore, it's imperative that educators continue to have input. You can take the following actions in the short term to help you understand what students need while supporting educators as they implement changes to facilitate student engagement.

- **Listen to student voices.** What opportunities have students had to share their perspectives on anti-racism and related topics? In addition to quantitative data, seek student stories and perspectives as data to inform decisions. Students encounter racism from adults and peers, and they exhibit racial biases themselves. These biases contribute to their academic experiences, sense of belonging, self-efficacy, and interpersonal relationships. Create intentional times to listen to and learn from students. You can provide space for these efforts via interviews, focus groups, surveys, and class discussions. By amplifying student voices and creating safe spaces to share, you can help students engage in activities that meet their needs more specifically.

- **Gauge family support.** Do families in your school's community support anti-racist efforts? Are they talking about race at home with their children? What is their understanding of DEI work? As you plan ways to engage students more directly, it's good practice to make families aware and gather an understanding of how families may already be approaching related topics. Of course, you could get various responses and levels of support, but it's best to be transparent about your work and welcome discussions. You may have unsupportive families. In these situations, you can still listen to understand the root of different opinions and use this to inform your messaging. What exactly do people disagree with, and what information can you share to help families understand the motivation and purpose of DEI and anti-racist work? This need is another reason to have data that supports your actions. Additionally, if you have families that voice their support, uplift and amplify those voices.

- **Take inventory of what's already being done to directly support students through an anti-racist lens.** As you think about ways to engage students directly, consider what supports, resources, and activities are already offered. Efforts connected to equity goals might already be in place and need extra support and strategic thinking. Find out what already exists and connect with the educators in charge to learn what has been working well and what challenges they have faced. Whether you're looking at student groups, curriculum audits, or other activities, learning about this work provides insight into where you have opportunities to strengthen the support provided to students.

- **Solicit teacher input.** Connect with teachers to hear their perspectives on what supports students will benefit from. For example, if a teacher shares that they have many student conflicts, and your school has invested time into learning about strategies such as restorative practices, then consider how to create student groups or facilitate positive connections between students. By working with teachers to gain a deeper understanding of the challenges students face, you and your team can be more intentional about your efforts to support students through an anti-racist lens.

A BLUEPRINT FOR FULL IMPLEMENTATION

Step 1: Gather data to determine student needs.

You may have started talking with students to better understand their experiences and sense of belonging in your school. Work with the committee or team leading anti-racist efforts to plan for how you'll reach out to other stakeholders such as families and teachers. The goal is to understand what students encounter regarding their identity in classrooms and peer-to-peer relationships, along with their sense of self-efficacy and value. When you begin connecting with stakeholders, especially students, look for common themes or patterns to guide decision-making about what direct support students would benefit from the most. The data will inform how you move forward to support students. Here are examples of what those supports could look like:

- facilitating brave spaces for student discourse
- creating affinity groups
- increasing access to resources such as texts and other connections to learn about race and cultural identity
- developing a process for supporting students who disclose, or want to disclose, incidents of bias with peers or teachers
- updating or changing curriculum to center perspectives and experiences from historically marginalized communities

Step 2: Plan for the 5 W's.

Consider the what, why, who, where, and when regarding encouraging student participation in anti-racist work.

- *What* will you implement based on the information you gain from stakeholders, especially students? Determining the best way to directly engage students in anti-racist work could mean creating student groups with focuses such as learning about identity or affinity groups. Or it may require more input and expertise from staff and administration to take action, such as auditing the curriculum to make schoolwide or district-wide changes to instructional materials. Whatever you determine to be the most critical changes may necessitate various levels of involvement from staff, so you'll also want to consider what is feasible and sustainable and what is best for students.

- *Why* is this the best way to support students currently? Many factors contribute to how you and your team decide to support students. It depends on resources, staff capacity and availability, and family support, to name a few. No matter the factors, doing what is best for students and addressing racial equity concerns must be the driving force behind any decision. Create a mission statement or short pitch to share with stakeholders and express why this support for students is valuable and necessary and how it will benefit the school community.

- *Who* needs to be involved to make these plans happen? Consider these questions when determining who you may need to communicate with to bring the vision to life:
  - ▶ Will teachers need to facilitate?
  - ▶ Who has the skills and knowledge to ensure it will be a fruitful endeavor that does not cause harm?
  - ▶ Do guardians need to provide permission?
  - ▶ Does your school leadership support the plan?
  - ▶ Will you need to request funds or materials from anyone?
  - ▶ Are students involved in any capacity of facilitation?

> ▸ What type of space do you need, and what are the logistics of getting it?

- *Where* and *when* will this support take place? If you are planning an extracurricular activity during or after school, the "where and when" will depend on the availability of students, staff, transportation, and family/guardian permission, to name a few. Carefully consider all these factors to plan for the most engagement and sustainability.

Step 3: Obtain support from stakeholders.

At this point, you've gathered supporting data and created a plan to move forward. Now it's time to get input and share the plan with those impacted by these efforts, as well as stakeholders whose support you need to make it happen. Sharing is especially valuable if you need funding, school space, or facilitators. Using the plan you created in Step 2 and your short pitch, put together an easily digestible, motivating proposal for stakeholders so they can quickly understand what is being done to support students, and why. Depending on your audience (such as teachers, board members, and families), you might need to create multiple versions to meet the questions and concerns of each group. When you share with stakeholders, be prepared to receive feedback and questions. As with any new efforts, some may support how you intend to engage students, and some may not. While all feedback is important to consider for improvements, be discerning when considering input that does not prioritize what is best for students or help you further anti-racist efforts.

Step 4: Recruit and implement.

Now, it's time to bring these student engagement plans to fruition! Depending on the team's chosen initiative(s) and available means and support, implementation will look different at each school. If you need to recruit students or staff, what is your message? If student and staff input were foundational to organizing the efforts, then you already have a strong "why" to communicate to the intended audience in a way that encourages participation and commitment.

How will you encourage active participation from students? At every grade level, if these efforts are meant to directly support and benefit students, their reception, understanding, and interest must be a driving factor for how you implement and sustain the endeavor. Consider these questions:

- How will you know if students are benefiting? Will you collect data? Artifacts? Anecdotes?

- How will you ensure the plan is sustainable? How many people are supporting these efforts? If you are using school funds, is more funding secured for the future? Does scheduling permit continuing this effort?

With any endeavor, we must be forward-thinking in our execution to ensure the survival of our efforts to support students. Root changes within your school's systems and structures so they become part of the ecosystem and can be adapted or evolved as needed to survive. We want these changes to be long term and benefit students for years to come.

OVERCOMING PUSHBACK

Keep students at the center. As you and your team make changes to provide a more just education, you will have plenty of opinions and challenges. No matter what, keep students at the center. We must be willing to stand firm in our responsibility to do what is best for all students and find creative solutions to roadblocks as we make changes. Here are counterarguments you might hear and how you can respond.

WE WANT THESE CHANGES TO BE LONG TERM AND BENEFIT STUDENTS FOR YEARS TO COME.

Involving students in conversations about racism and identity is indoctrination. Children as young as three to five not only recognize race but also develop racial bias, a fact shared by Erin Winkler in "Children are not colorblind: How young children learn race." As much as adults would like to protect children from ugly truths about racism, the unfortunate fact is that many students of color suffer from racism at young ages, and both white students and students of color have perpetuated racist beliefs. If children are old enough to experience racism, then they deserve safe ways to develop a deeper understanding of race, become aware of their identities, share their stories, and discuss the history behind it all.

Bias, prejudice, discrimination, and racism all exist and contribute to students' experiences in and out of school, as well as their identity development and sense of self-worth as they grow up. Imagine schools as places where educators are equipped with the skills to facilitate these conversations and where students are encouraged to think critically about race and identity. Being supported in these conversations builds empathy, understanding, and greater self-awareness. Rather than creating division, engaging in anti-racist learning empowers students to better understand themselves and the world around them. Adults may be weary of teaching historically accurate accounts of some of our nation's darkest moments and believe the myth that this creates division and hate. However, equipped with information and a true understanding of the ways that race permeates our society, students will instead be empowered to disrupt societal norms that continue to perpetuate disparities between BIPOC and white students.

Change will take time; let's focus on professional development first. Does change take time? Absolutely. But, as your school develops teachers' capacities to support anti-racist teaching and learning, the change can benefit students. Prioritizing student needs and making connections to adult learning are powerful ways to begin seeing changes that continue to develop teacher mindsets and practices and begin to impact students' success, which is the top goal. Additionally, intentionally planning ways to directly engage students in anti-racist efforts will help to build the bridge between theory and practice. When educators learn new strategies and practices, it can be difficult to recognize or create moments when they know how to apply what they've learned. By intentionally creating and facilitating these opportunities for students, both students and adults are learning.

We don't have the money (or other resources) to do this. This is a valid concern if you need materials or other resources. However, it doesn't mean abandoning plans to engage students. Collaborate with your team to think about the main purpose of your plan for student engagement (i.e., providing resources or an after-school club) and how you can work together to revise the plan so you can still achieve this purpose. Also consider who, if anyone, has the power to help you attain what you need. Have you developed relationships with anyone who might be able to help you secure the resources to move forward? Engaging students is a necessary part of anti-racist teaching and learning. So, when you face challenges, it's okay to reimagine what this engagement will look like.

THE HACK IN ACTION

In Hack 2, I detailed the creation of a school's Equity Committee that collaborated to create goals promoting racial equity within the school. The goals were:

> Goal 1: Increase awareness and involvement of families and students in relation to the school's focus on equity.
>
> Goal 2: Provide grade-level-appropriate, racial-equity-related lessons and resources to staff.

During the first year of the committee, we focused on creating schoolwide opportunities for students to engage in learning about racial and ethnic diversity and history. In alignment with both goals, we started with schoolwide research projects for Hispanic Heritage Month and Black History Month. We also created resource folders that staff could utilize year-round. These folders provided materials for teachers so they had access to supplemental activities and other resources they could offer directly to students. Although these projects were great ways to start involving students in more conversations about culture and identity, our committee needed to know how each classroom approached the research project and the quality or depth of their conversations about the topics. Most classes participated in producing an artifact to add to a school display, but the product only sometimes represented the process. For projects focused on racial and cultural identities, the discussions and learning that we hoped would take place were the most significant pieces of the process. At the end of that year, the committee decided it would be beneficial to engage students more directly.

While we would continue offering schoolwide activities, we wanted to engage students in more direct learning about race, identity, and equity. Before the school year ended, the committee designed a plan for an after-school club that would focus on these topics and still align with our committee goals, which we had developed based on the school's data. We created a one-pager that detailed the club's mission and the 5 W's by answering these questions:

- *Who* will be in the after-school club: specific grade levels or all grades? Will joining the club be voluntary or by nomination? Who will facilitate the club? Who do we need to communicate with—parents, staff, and administrators? Who do we need permission from?
- *What* is our focus each time we meet? What resources and materials do we need?
- *When* will we meet?
- *Where* will we meet?
- *Why* is the club needed, and what is our purpose?
- Mission Statement: "Students will meet to discuss and learn about elementary-appropriate equity-related topics. This will be done with the purpose of increasing their awareness and knowledge of racial equity within our school and community. Students will become actively involved in our school community by engaging in their new role as Equity Ambassadors."

We drafted the one-pager with the intention of sharing it with our principal and director of equity and instruction for their feedback and support. Later, this document would be a foundational piece when detailing the club's purpose for all stakeholders. The group would be the first of its kind at the elementary level, while secondary grades were already engaging in these conversations in extracurricular activities. Moving forward, we would partner with another elementary school to pilot the club so we could share ideas and discuss the impact on students.

The final step before the school year ended was to curate a list of materials for purchase, thanks to the support of the director of equity and instruction. All this planning took place prior to the end of the school year, with the intention of starting the club at the

Get Students Engaged

beginning of the following school year. This timeline gave facilitators a chance to work together to thoughtfully plan the objective for each session and select the materials and resources they needed. At the beginning of the new school year, we shared the club's mission with the school staff and families to begin signing up students. Since the group would take place after school, we had to make sure families knew that transportation was not provided and confirm emergency contact information. We also distributed the list of meeting dates so families could plan transportation ahead of time if needed.

During our first Equity Ambassador Club meeting, Rachel and I, who facilitated the club, taught students about the difference between equity and equality—most were only familiar with equality—and guided students to create Identity Webs. See Image 3 for an example.

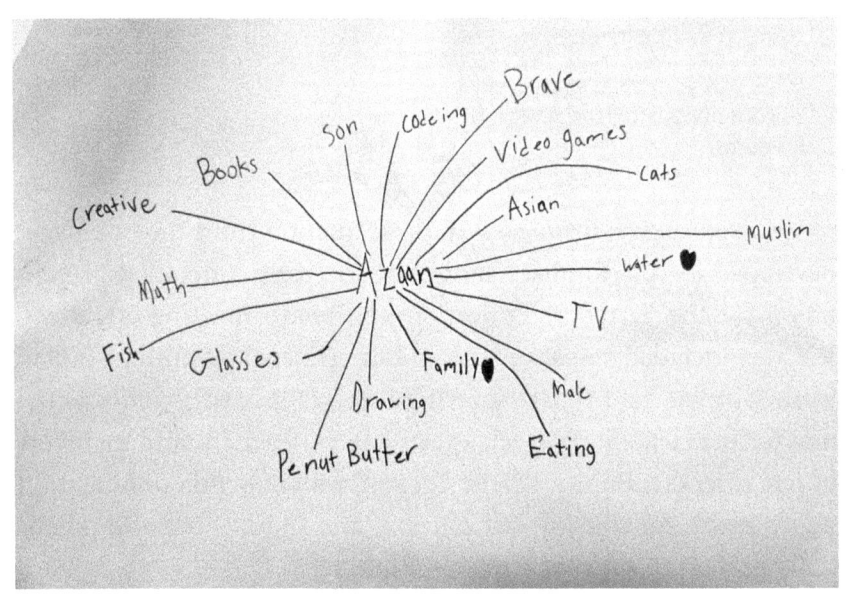

Image 3: An example of a student identity web.

Right before this first meeting, we were asked to share a presentation about the student club with the Board of Education. With this in mind, we distributed a survey to families and students at the end of the first meeting. We wanted to include the voices of our students and families who were expressing their perspectives in support of why this direct engagement of students in racial equity work was meaningful.

Questions we asked parents:	Questions we asked students:
How would you describe equity?	How do you feel about today's first meeting, and why?
Do you feel that equity is important for your child's success?	What would you like to learn from participating in the club?
Using this definition of equity—"Equity is giving everyone what they need to succeed"—what do you hope your child will get out of being in the Equity Club?	Is there anything you would like us to know about you?
What was your child's response or comments after the first club meeting?	

We used survey responses and information from the one-pager developed by the Equity Committee to create a detailed presentation for the Board of Education and board meeting attendees. We also included steps we took in our strategic planning, student work samples, and future meeting topics. Since this club was the first for the elementary level, as facilitators, teachers, and members of our district's Equity Leaders group, we knew this presentation was valuable for sharing our purpose and significance and potentially garnering support for it to continue.

As students met throughout the school year, participating in activities to learn about various topics related to race and identity, my co-facilitator and I debriefed after each meeting to discuss student engagement and learning, revising upcoming plans as needed.

We collected student artifacts and shared how the work was going with our partner elementary school, principal, and director of equity and instruction. As we neared the final meeting, we took time to reflect on how the club progressed over the course of the school year. We discussed these questions and more:

- Were there scheduling conflicts that lowered attendance?
- Do we change the process for students joining the club?
- How feasible was bi-weekly facilitation with two teachers? Do we need to make any changes?
- What were students most engaged by?
- What did students learn, and how do we know?
- What were the families' overall understanding and perspective of the club?
- Did they feel it was meaningful in their child's development during the school year?
- What materials or resources were most and least useful?

As with any new initiative, we knew we needed to make changes to strengthen the work. We also made an effort to collect student feedback.

Students shared that they enjoyed:

- writing about their feelings
- learning what equity means
- doing lots of drawing and learning about themselves and others
- trying new things

Students shared that they learned:

- equity means everyone gets what they need
- about believing in themselves
- to call people by their correct name
- about bias
- to be yourself and not change for others
- that everyone is unique and different

While this club engaged a small number of students from our school's population, it was a truly diverse group (racially, ethnically, linguistically, academically, and ability-wise). It encouraged students to develop their understanding of identity and increased their sense of self-awareness and self-efficacy. They engaged in conversations that required empathy for those with different experiences and a level of honesty about challenging interactions they faced. They learned about bias and microaggressions, which are sometimes difficult for adults to understand. These students did not leave our club divided but with a deeper understanding of themselves and the world around them. They also practiced the language to discuss emotionally challenging situations. They left with tools to be empowered to speak up for themselves and support others when needed, which is critical to moving toward a more just and anti-racist society.

With the possibility of so many valuable yet differing opinions from different stakeholders, we must remain guided by our focus on doing what is best for students. By engaging students in conversations and activities related to anti-racism and DEI work, we uplift student voices and create avenues for them to share their experiences and connect. The students we serve today are the changemakers of tomorrow. If they have a better understanding of their own identities and the world around them, we can create a more supportive, affirming environment within the school. They will be prepared for the future by having a greater critical consciousness and the confidence to advocate for themselves and others.

HACK 7

INVITE FAMILY PARTICIPATION
WELCOME FAMILIES INTO THE SCHOOL COMMUNITY

Do the best you can until you know better.
Then when you know better, do better.
— MAYA ANGELOU, AUTHOR, SCHOLAR, AND CIVIL RIGHTS ACTIVIST

THE PROBLEM: IT IS DIFFICULT TO GET FAMILIES ENGAGED

ONE CHALLENGE THAT schools and educators often have when implementing changes to be more culturally responsive is family involvement and engagement. Families are partners in their child's education. When schools and families work together, they can better provide an education that more holistically meets the needs of students. A common problem in some communities is low family participation in school activities. In other communities where families are more involved, it may be difficult to convince them that anti-racist teaching and learning is what is best for all students.

Family responses and involvement in the school vary based on many factors. In communities where the staff does not reflect the demographics of the community, it can result in deep misunderstandings about the beliefs, culture, and customs of the families. Additionally, classism and racism play a role when staff members hold certain biases and prejudices about the families they serve. Without intentional education and learning, they may also lack an understanding of the societal issues that affect families within the community, such as environmental injustices, education levels, and employment trends. Other factors such as occasions for involvement, the history of the community, and the historical relationship with the school as a hub of the community also play a role in the participation of families.

THE HACK: INVITE FAMILY PARTICIPATION

Families are integral to students' experiences in school. From providing enriching activities, supporting emotional development, and offering academic guidance, family involvement in a student's life is one of the key factors in student success. In "Reframing Family Involvement in Education: Supporting Families to Support Educational Equity," Weiss et al. discuss the family and school connection, building relationships, and communication of meaningful information—all of which results in children doing better in school. The goal of working intentionally with families is critical for the achievement of all students.

When educators create and welcome opportunities to connect with families, they can develop a deeper understanding of each student's history, family background, and frame of reference that influences how they perceive school, learning, and relationships. We also gain a more complex understanding of who the student is and how we can collaborate with their family to meet their needs and provide the family with resources to support the student. If we do not get to know the families we work with or offer ways for them to get to know the school and educators, it can lead to a misunderstanding and a lack of communication. Without family connections on various levels—through teachers and support staff, event engagement, and feedback on decision-making—how can we ensure that we are truly doing what is best for students? Consequently, this allows biases, prejudices, and assumptions to fabricate the whole picture and deliver poorly informed decisions that impact students.

In schools that serve mostly Black, Indigenous, people of color, and low-income communities (though not limited to these communities), this is a long-standing problem. Lack of translation services, mental and physical health differences, unreliable transportation, limitations placed on parents and guardians by employers, cultural incongruences, lack of educational opportunities about school policies and procedures, and even a family's own negative experiences with schooling are all factors that create barriers to involvement. It is critical to note that these issues often stem from continued systemic racism. Schools can work to alleviate barriers and stop the harmful narrative that parents don't care enough to be involved when, in fact, many other factors are at play that create barriers to involvement.

While increasing family involvement is a commonly shared commitment in schools, efforts and support to engage families vary greatly, as well as family responsiveness. In communities with strong engagement, the challenge might be to garner family support for changes that address social justice issues. Some families may view conversations around social justice issues as the responsibility of the adults at home. However, issues such as racism affect students' lives at school and the community at large. Not only is school an integral part of the community, but it is a school's responsibility to educate the whole child and prepare them to be successful when they leave the school building. Students come to school as their whole selves, and educators are tasked with the hard job of meeting their instructional needs and their social and emotional needs to create an environment that is safe and conducive to learning for every child.

Doing this well requires educators to prioritize inclusivity and seek support from families. By providing families with various methods of connection, resources, and intentional engagement, we can increase family involvement. Through welcoming each family's perspectives, looking closely at their needs, and offering ways to get involved in school life and anti-racist efforts, we can help families understand the "why" behind this value and gain their trust to push progress forward and support the child's learning.

> **NOT ONLY IS SCHOOL AN INTEGRAL PART OF THE COMMUNITY, BUT IT IS A SCHOOL'S RESPONSIBILITY TO EDUCATE THE WHOLE CHILD AND PREPARE THEM TO BE SUCCESSFUL WHEN THEY LEAVE THE SCHOOL BUILDING.**

WHAT YOU CAN DO TOMORROW

Building relationships with families is essential to understanding and supporting students. How we develop relationships needs to be grounded in authentic desires to get to know families and children, as well as intentional actions. We can strive to let go of assumptions and get to know families for who they are if we aim to meet their children's needs to the best of our ability. Here are actions you can take right away.

- **Gain a general understanding of the various backgrounds and families represented within your school.** Take a moment to reflect. What do you know about the families of your students? What do teachers know about their students' families, and what efforts have been made to learn more? What data is available? Two short-term actions you can take are to:
    1. Look into family surveys that have been given to garner family opinions, experiences, and dynamics (or consider creating one). These surveys can provide enlightening details that are key to determining the next steps and planning for family engagement.
    2. Look for data that is already available:
        - demographic data
        - behavioral data
        - attendance data

        While this information is specifically about students and does not provide a fully informed picture of the family unit, it can give you a starting place so you can reach out and build closer relationships with them. Later, you can use this information to inform your actions to get families more involved.
- **Reach out to families of "extreme users."** What do you know about the "extreme users" within your school? These are the students and families who

maximize the use of the educational services, compared to most students who can achieve average success with mainstream services. For example, extreme users are the students who have not been able to remain in traditional classroom settings, utilize services such as special education or counseling, are chronically absent, present the most challenging behaviors, struggle academically, are most disengaged with school, and fall into other categories of those who require more support services. As described by Bethan Phillimore in "The Fundamentals of Engaging with Extreme Users," a design-thinking approach is where changes are user-centered and empathy-driven; you design changes and solutions based on the user's experiences in order to better meet their needs. Reaching out to learn more about these students and their families helps educators understand what school or community resources students and families need to be successful and develop more targeted engagement strategies.

- **Evaluate what services, resources, and opportunities for involvement your school offers.** What opportunities for involvement have been offered, and have they been successful? Depending on how communication has historically been shared with families, developing a deeper understanding of this may be as simple as looking through your school's communication applications or as tedious as surveying families and staff. Either way, gathering information about what has been done in the past helps inform what will be effective in the future. Ask these questions to determine the effectiveness of existing engagement opportunities:

- ▸ Why was this opportunity chosen?
- ▸ Did families utilize the opportunity?
- ▸ Was the opportunity specific to their needs? If not, what was the purpose?
- ▸ Was there any follow-up with families after the opportunity was shared or after they participated?

- **Survey staff to learn more about the most and least successful communication methods.** For many families, teachers are the main source of communication and connection to a school. Therefore, teachers may be able to provide a more informed perspective on how to connect with families most effectively. Methods of communication are a critical factor in family engagement. If you can get an idea of the most effective way to get in touch, on an individual or schoolwide basis, you can determine the best methods to communicate options for engagement. With technology providing so many ways to interact with families, this is a critical factor to consider when thinking about the most effective methods of connection that will lead to family engagement.

A BLUEPRINT FOR FULL IMPLEMENTATION

Step 1: Develop a shared definition of family engagement and involvement.

Developing a shared definition of key focuses, such as family involvement, helps to ensure a clearer understanding of expectations and establish a foundational definition of what is meant when discussing family involvement. Your leadership team or school community at large can collaborate to develop a shared definition of family involvement or engagement that reflects the needs of your community, is inclusive, and recognizes the nuances of "involvement." This shared definition can acknowledge the value of school-based, community-based, and home-based support and involvement in education. Schools can and should appreciate that engagement is not limited to attendance at school events and conferences. Families can also support their child's education at home and through community networks by utilizing offered school and community resources.

Step 2: Increase school and staff capacity to engage families in meaningful, affirming ways.

It's crucial to grow your school's professional capacity so staff has the tools to meet expectations and change their practices. In my work as a teacher, communication with families was an integral part of education. Being able to communicate effectively and build relationships takes skills that we need to develop, along with empathy gained from listening and learning. As you think about ways to engage families, consider staff beliefs about students and families. If anti-racism is a true value, then we must unpack and address our beliefs and assumptions about the families we serve.

A multitude of societal and systemic factors impact family engagement, particularly in schools serving socioeconomically disadvantaged and predominantly BIPOC communities. Nonetheless, it is common to hear the rhetoric of "They don't care about their child" or "They don't value education," assuming a lack of motivation or desire to be involved in their child's education. If teachers hold these beliefs about parents and families, there is no doubt that this bias and deficit thinking shows up in how they communicate with families. (To learn more about this topic, check out the book *Hacking Deficit Thinking* by Byron McClure and Kelsie Reed.) It is not enough to simply expect staff to communicate with families. We can also interrogate how we develop a deeper sense of empathy and understanding to have meaningful, respectful communication that meets families' needs without placing blame or promoting harmful narratives. We can do this by providing staff with resources and professional learning on more culturally responsive family engagement. Ideally, this will include:

- Learning about the history of the community and populations served. What historical context (such as racism and classism) might affect relationships between local schools and families?

- Learning about the cultures and cultural norms of the community and being mindful that cultural and ethnic diversity exists within all racial categories.

- Learning what languages families speak and offering resources for translation services and interpreters (not relying on students to interpret).

- Understanding challenges around involvement for migrant and immigrant families and possible fears for undocumented families.

- Learning about the challenges that single-parent families, extended-family guardians, and marginalized families face.
- Providing opportunities for professional learning on communication and relationship-building with families. As mentioned, effective communication is a skill. Through our communication, we consciously and subconsciously communicate our beliefs and feelings about students and families. If we want all families to feel welcome and as though they are partners in education, then we must be intentional in our actions. Here are suggestions for professional learning:
    - ▶ Establish positive relationships: One of the many things I learned as an undergraduate in the Neag School of Education at the University of Connecticut was the importance of building positive relationships with families. It was recommended never to let the first contact be a negative one. One way to do this is to make it a goal to call every parent or guardian during the first month of school to introduce yourself and share something positive. What a great piece of advice to begin positive communication with families, especially those with whom I'd be in frequent contact throughout the year due to behavioral or academic concerns. I also made it a point to contact families and share positive news after we had to discuss something heavy like challenging behavior. It was a way to "replenish" our relationship.
    - ▶ Work on anti-bias behaviors: I recall a time when a parent came late for a conference and expressed to me that, as he was on his way to my classroom,

a colleague looked him up and down and asked him why he was there in a way he felt was condescending. He was wearing a worn T-shirt and ripped jeans and had his skateboard. Whether intended or not, he felt frustrated and put down. Every individual deserves to be treated with respect, regardless of how they present. Offering training around biases can help us recognize when our biases impact communication and family relationships.

- ▸ Avoid making assumptions: As humans, it is hard not to make assumptions. However, they influence our interactions and relationships. Like everyone else, I have been guilty of making negative assumptions about a family's involvement, especially with students I felt challenged by. However, over time, I've learned to assume one thing: Everyone is doing the best they can. For me, this shifted the way I approached relationships with parents and guardians and allowed me to focus on how I could be of assistance rather than placing judgment on people and situations whose experiences lay outside the scope of my understanding. Establishing this belief requires a change in mindset, but it is a belief that helps us extend more grace and empathy and be a better support to the families we work with.

Step 3: Equip staff with methods to learn more about families.

While academic performance and behavioral history are significant pieces of information, so is everything else about who a student is. Ask yourself how educators and the school are learning more about students to inform the pedagogy, practices, and environment. As a teacher, I sent a survey home to families at the start of every school year, and the results helped me learn more about their children. The survey provided the following information about students:

- holidays they do and do not celebrate
- who the child lives with or other family dynamics their guardian felt were important to share
- what their child enjoys and feels challenged by, whether school-related or not
- what motivates and upsets their child
- languages spoken at home
- primary contact person and best method of contact
- interest in school events or parent groups

If creating or sharing a survey with families at your school, brainstorm other questions that would help staff gain insights into the specific needs of your students and families. Whether through a survey or phone call, intentionally learn more about the families that make up your school community. Later, this information will inform the relationships you build with families and students and guide planning for engagement and resources that will most benefit families. Of course, there's the question of what to do if you don't get a reply after you've sent a survey, called, or texted. When I've had this happen, I still send communication whenever needed about academics, behavior, or otherwise. It can be deflating and frustrating not to receive a response, but if they see the messages and, at some point, decide to respond, I want them to know I still welcome the communication and relationship. In a practical sense, this is valuable if there's ever a need to provide documentation of attempts to communicate about their child.

Step 4: Plan for ways to increase involvement and transparency.

Earlier, I recommended getting to know the students and families who are extreme users. Learning more about these students and families enables you to take a more intentional and meaningful approach to planning. Don't just think about what is in the school's capacity to *do*, but also focus on what families *need* in order to be more involved and what they can *bring into* the school community. If your school's definition of family involvement is inclusive of the ways that families support their child's education at home and through community organizations, then you can plan for opportunities that go beyond school-based events. Remember that learning also takes place outside of school, and if we can offer ways to promote learning in any capacity, we have a better chance of meeting students' needs. Here are ideas for engagement:

- Encourage families' capacity to support and advocate for students by offering learning opportunities about:
    - content-specific academic resources for teaching and learning at home
    - educational jargon
    - services such as special education, English learner programs, academic and behavioral intervention processes, and other supports
- Share community resources, such as:
    - information about local organizations that offer resources (youth centers, libraries, faith-based organizations)
    - organizations to partner with to host events or offer other materials and resources

- Make targeted efforts to address societal barriers, such as housing, transportation, food insecurity, and childcare, by:
    - partnering with community members and leaders who have relationships with families
    - creating a central place for families to find resources offered by the school and local organizations
- Find opportunities for involvement and transparency with anti-racist efforts through:
    - special events at school or in the community to celebrate cultures and facilitate discourse
    - gatherings for families to share about their identities
    - resources and materials for families to continue learning and discussing at home
    - newsletters or other materials on related topics and current happenings at school
- Listen and learn from families via:
    - home visits (after completing training)
    - school and community discussion forums
    - family surveys
    - parent leadership and participation on boards and committees

OVERCOMING PUSHBACK

Working with families is one of the most valuable yet difficult responsibilities of being an educator. Every family has its own stories, needs, and opinions; as educators, we must engage them all, regardless of our preparation. While we will be challenged, we can also find solutions to meet the broad needs of families within our school community and engage them in meaningful and beneficial ways. Here are possible objections and responses.

We don't have time to make calls and connections. We all know that teachers have limited time. One common complaint I've heard from educators is that the time designated for preparation is not long enough and gets filled with meetings or covering classes. As difficult as it can be, we must protect our preparation time. For educators to be the best teachers they can be, they need a healthy work-life balance, which means not being expected to sacrifice their personal time to complete work-related tasks. Sure, we often do it when we have to, but this habit contributes to stress and burnout.

> **EVERY FAMILY HAS ITS OWN STORIES, NEEDS, AND OPINIONS; AS EDUCATORS, WE MUST ENGAGE THEM ALL, REGARDLESS OF OUR PREPARATION.**

If you are a school leader, consider what systems and structures you can implement so educators have time during the school day to contact families. Additionally, family communication can go beyond phone calls. As a teacher, I learned that many families preferred to receive messages, and I benefited from using a schoolwide messaging system. For parents and guardians who did not utilize the schoolwide application, or whenever I preferred to make a phone call, I used a web-based phone number to call and text. This was a game-changer! Sometimes, the ease of completing a task comes down to the tools available. Ensure that educators are aware of the various technological resources that can make family communication more efficient. Other methods of communication include periodical posts using an online platform and digital or printed newsletters from the school or teachers. These are options for educators to communicate regularly with families, but they are not the only methods and do not replace personal connections.

We don't have the resources and funding to do all these things. I often hear this common concern, and my advice remains: Do what you can within your means. Also, seek out free resources and options for funding. If consistent, reliable communication is an issue, look into free technology applications teachers can use. If building positive relationships is a concern, utilize the leadership team to learn about the factors specific to your community that influence trust, and provide in-house professional learning. If you need money to organize family events, what creative fundraisers can you plan? Sometimes, the barriers to involvement are not about monetary resources but relationships. If families are facing barriers like transportation or translation, are there community networks that can help? Be willing to develop connections with community organizations and ask for support. Importantly, keep in mind that engaging families does not always necessitate heavy spending, and families also have a lot to offer. Get creative when thinking about how your school can organize low-cost events and opportunities for engagement where members of the school community contribute.

Parents and families are not educational experts. Families may or may not be knowledgeable about the field of education, but most are experts on their own children. Working to engage and include families does not mean expecting them to propose or debate decisions, but schools can include them in the decision-making process when appropriate, as well as provide opportunities to increase their capacity to make informed decisions about their children's education.

In communities where families are engaged and vocal about decisions, it is critical for schools to be transparent and also stand firm in choices made to support all students. Everybody has opinions and beliefs, and some families have strong opinions about topics related to race, social justice, and equity. However, our duty as educators is to make informed decisions that will help all students achieve academic success and be holistically supported as individuals. We can never please everyone. In an anti-racist school, this means that we must be ready for backlash and fight for what is right for students by working with families and the community to share knowledge and the rationale for decisions. This work will help some folks understand the "why" behind anti-racism, and we must also accept that some families hold fast to racist beliefs and are not willing to support these efforts. We cannot change everyone's views, but we can work within our sphere of influence to change what we can and make a difference for students. Do not let naysayers stop progress.

THE HACK IN ACTION

Natalie Holz is a director of equity and inclusion at Heartley Academy, an independent Catholic kindergarten through eighth-grade school. She has worked as an educator for twenty years, most recently as a diversity, equity, and inclusion practitioner. The independent school she currently serves is located in a large urban area with a racially, linguistically, economically, and religiously diverse population of families—a feature that contradicts stereotypical, preconceived notions of what it means to be an independent religious school. Natalie's school has made efforts to learn about the families it serves, listen and respond to families' needs, and develop the capacity of educators to support families in the most meaningful ways.

As in many schools, it has taken time to learn and understand what works for Natalie's community and how to continually evolve and improve. One way they learned about their community is by collecting demographic data that allows families to self-identify and share information about who they are, which helps the school establish a more accurate picture of who they serve and how they can support families and teachers. For example, this data underpinned efforts to recognize the multilingualism of their community and how they approach communication with families. Knowing that more than thirty languages are spoken across student homes has shaped teacher practices.

In preparation for parent-teacher conferences, Natalie attended teacher-team meetings to talk about communication with families who have limited English proficiency. In these conversations, she found it was often assumed that if a family was quiet during a conference, it meant that they did not understand what was being discussed. Natalie and the teachers unpacked this assumption and took another more productive and responsive approach. They began the practice of scripting what they wanted to say before the conference to become more mindful of the language being used. They also sent talking points to families ahead of the meeting so they could have more time to process. Natalie recognized the importance of giving practical skills to teachers and talking about the assumptions they made instead of ignoring how they could be harmful. They needed to understand that our assumptions about families can keep them from being involved.

Other efforts to engage families have been motivated by the powerful yet sometimes underrated action of simply asking and listening. At the beginning of the school year, teachers put much effort into learning about the students and their families and finding ways to incorporate what they've learned. The school can then use this information to inform decisions. An example of this is how Heartley revised its approach to holidays.

As a Catholic school, during December, the school would engage in Christmas activities and welcome families to share what they celebrate during the December holiday season. However, as they learned that not everyone celebrates during this time, and their campus became more religiously diverse, they found other ways to include and uplift the various practices of different families. Through a group effort, the campus minister incorporated the variety of religions represented on their campus and their significant dates into the daily prayer binder. Families were also surveyed at the beginning of the year and invited to pick a time to come into the school and share about a holiday their family celebrates. Natalie noticed that families are receptive to the invitation to share about their cultures, which translated into involvement with planning field trips for students. For example, families worked together to plan a field trip to a Hindu temple for an entire grade level. Natalie believes that these events make families feel that they can add something to the school, and as a result, it enhances the education of all students.

Another shift their school made was in their approach to Halloween. Heartley serves a large population of East African students who practice many different religions and do not celebrate Halloween. The school noticed many students would stay home on Halloween due to the activities. In response, the school asked families what it could offer so students did not have to stay home and miss school. Subsequently, during classroom Halloween parties, Heartley began offering another space with a fall festival as an activity choice. Although attendance at the fall festival began with only one student, they engaged room parents in reaching out to families and letting them know there would be an alternate choice with crafts and activities for those who do not celebrate Halloween. The school also worked with teachers to adjust the curriculum on Halloween to include more activity and assignment choices. In the year following the first fall festival, the number of students attending increased to fourteen. Natalie found that by simply asking families what they needed and wanted and how they could meet that need, the school could create solutions for families to feel increasingly comfortable sending their children to school on Halloween.

In addition to being responsive to the cultures and practices of their community, Heartley has also become more intentional about increasing the diversity of parents in leadership roles. The school noticed that within the Parent Teacher Association (PTA), many wealthy families had at least one stay-at-home parent who could join the PTA. These families were predominantly white, which created a predominantly white PTA that did not reflect the diversity of their community. As a response, Natalie and others at the school strived to increase the group's diversity so all members of their community were represented. They also ensured that the individuals in charge of recruiting room parents supported anti-racist efforts and would take intentional actions that reflected this, and, in turn, the parents they recruited would support the school's vision.

Additionally, the school strategically used community engagement events, such as their International Night, to connect with families and enlist their leadership skills. The event started small and grew to host over six hundred people. During International Night, many of the school's immigrant families would attend to connect and meet each other. Now, the school also uses this time to recruit parents into leadership roles.

International Night is Heartley's biggest family event organized by the Equity and Inclusion Council, a parent committee. For such a major community-building event, it comes with a low cost for the school. They provide the event space and paper goods for eating, and the families bring dishes for a potluck-style dinner. By talking with families, they learned that people just wanted a place to come together; they didn't need keynote speakers, dancers, and other activities that would make this a high-cost event and more difficult to organize. People weren't attending for the entertainment; they went because it was a place where they felt they belonged. Over time, the school revised the messaging and invitation—including a push to have students invite their friends—and families shifted from viewing the event as a space primarily for immigrant families to viewing it as an event for all to come together and celebrate diversity and connection as a community.

The ways that Natalie's school has approached family engagement reflect a willingness to listen, learn, and grow. As they grew to understand the families they served, they made changes to better meet their needs and, importantly, strategically invited families into leadership positions. Nevertheless, this work has not been without its challenges. One of the greatest challenges has been developing a stronger asset-based thinking practice among teachers. Natalie recognized instances where deficit thinking and negative assumptions about what families are capable of and their interest in involvement impacted communication and the outcome of situations. To combat this, they addressed and unpacked assumptions to help staff understand that everyone has something to offer. Whether this looks like a family visiting a class and teaching the students about their culture or a parent becoming a leader in the community, the school finds ways to get to know families and for them to feel that their voice matters and they're heard.

Another challenge is the constraint of time. Families are busy! Natalie noticed that while families wanted to be involved, the school needed to find ways to spread leadership responsibilities and create alternate engagement methods. One result was to offer more options for families to communicate, such as holding meetings on video conference platforms so they didn't have to take time off from work. Now, parent-teacher conferences and parent-organization meetings are held online, and more people can attend. For the parent organization, this resulted in a more diverse group of attendees.

While Heartley has made great strides in how families engage, Natalie would like to see continued growth in the way the school invites and amplifies parent-generated ideas, in addition to having a deeper understanding of which events are more popular or needed within different pockets of the community. As the school continues to grow and improve, Natalie plans to continue supporting staff by reflecting on the outcome of their behavior on family involvement, as well as being intentional about making personal connections with families so they know the school values who they are and what they have to offer.

Family engagement is a critical part of the school experience. From how we get to know the families we serve to the opportunities we plan for engagement, we must keep the needs of the community we serve at the center of our decision-making. As each child has so much to offer, so does each family. As we get to know who they are, we can create events that meet their needs and encourage them to contribute to the unique fabric of the school community.

HACK 8

PLAN FOR LONGEVITY
CREATE A FRAMEWORK SO THESE EFFORTS WILL LAST

Education is for improving the lives of others and for leaving your community and world better than you found it.
– MARIAN WRIGHT EDELMAN, ACTIVIST FOR
CIVIL RIGHTS AND CHILDREN'S RIGHTS

THE PROBLEM: CHANGES ARE HARD TO SUSTAIN

THROUGHOUT EACH HACK, I've offered guidance about effective practices and strategies and how to implement them rooted in your school's structures and systems. However, plenty of factors can affect how you make schoolwide changes and how effective they are. With leadership and staff transitions, fluctuating student and family needs, and resources that vary year to year, sustainability and consistency are real concerns. It can be difficult to ensure that changes survive over time. Add to this the changing tides of the educational landscape with the influence of new research, legal decisions, political elections, and national trends in education, and you have a variety of factors that impact students. As educators, we must continually evolve to respond to new information and opinions.

While some of this work can have a noticeable positive effect through improved practices and protecting student rights, we must also ensure that we continue to make anti-racism the foundation of future decisions and choices. If we treat anti-racism as another educational trend, fail to establish systemic or structural changes, compartmentalize anti-racist work, or follow the whim of inexperienced individuals who have no background in education, then efforts will evaporate and students, families, and entire communities will continue to pay the price. Time and again, reports on student achievement demonstrate racial inequity. We cannot continue to do what we have always done and expect results to be different. We must recognize the opportunity gaps students face and make changes that educators can sustain long into the future.

THE HACK: PLAN FOR LONGEVITY

Fostering a school environment that lives out the mission and foundational lens of anti-racism through all its values and actions does not happen overnight or even in a single school year. It takes intentional time because it requires a willingness to engage in personal growth on the part of educators, the development of professional capacity, and a determination to make structural and systemic changes. A great danger to progress can be the threat of abandoning efforts and the lack of maintaining or passing on integral institutional practices. It is crucial to intentionally plan for the longevity of any efforts made within the school's structures, systems, policies, and practices.

> **WE MUST RECOGNIZE THE OPPORTUNITY GAPS STUDENTS FACE AND MAKE CHANGES THAT EDUCATORS CAN SUSTAIN LONG INTO THE FUTURE.**

So, what does planning for longevity actually mean? It means we root the changes in evidence of need, create long-term goals, and provide the resources to support progress and ensure sustainability. As mentioned, many constantly changing factors in education require us to pivot. However, if we are committed to anti-racism, the efforts we make to improve teaching, learning, the climate, and the culture for all students need to be rooted in the systems and structures of the school. We must have a steadfast discernment when making changes in the name of progress to ensure they connect to the goals and values underpinning anti-racism and that resources, such as staff's professional capacity, can sustain them.

In my role as a diversity, equity, and inclusion practitioner, whenever I make decisions or changes, I contemplate the question, "What happens if I'm not here?" I'm always considering the sustainability of changes or programs to ensure that no matter who is leading the efforts, they are intentional in meeting the school's needs and can be carried on by others. Education environments include staff turnover and other changing factors, so if we want to see the long-term effect of racial equity work, we must treat it as a school value and not another passing trend; we need to engage in intentional, long-term planning that meets the specific needs of our schools.

WHAT YOU CAN DO TOMORROW

Planning for the longevity and continuity of efforts to create a more racially equitable school requires knowledge of the school and district's history and present-day efforts, as well as continued learning about practices and policies that create environments where all students can thrive and learn the skills to advocate for themselves and others. Here are a few actions you can take immediately as you plan for the changes to last.

- **Learn about previous staff experiences.** The educators in your building are the people who will be driving changes and connecting with students the most. Through their service, we can make changes to improve teaching, learning, the climate, and the culture. It is extremely helpful to know people's engagements and understandings of anti-racism, identity, and related topics. By creating avenues for staff to share their prior learning and experiences, you can use this information to inform goals and next steps. We must understand the professional capacity of the educators we work with so we can make moves that make sense and are realistic.

- **Seek examples of success from other schools.** Learning about successful programming in other schools can be helpful in jumpstarting ideas for your school. Many schools and districts create webpages dedicated to sharing about their diversity, equity, and inclusion work. Take time to look at other schools, both public and independent. Of course, we must be mindful that anyone can write anything on a webpage, and it doesn't tell the whole story; however, this can be a good approach to learning new ideas and ways to make a positive difference. I strongly believe that, as educators, if we find a resource or solution that is effective for students and makes a positive difference, and we share it and spread the wealth, we are working for the good of all students.

- **Make connections with peers involved in diversity, equity, and inclusion work.** If you find different ideas and practices that spark your curiosity about how they worked for other schools or how they got certain programs off the ground, reach out and make connections. As I've mentioned throughout this text, connecting with people who also value anti-racism and take actions to move toward racial equity is essential for our personal growth and emotional sustainability. Engaging in anti-racist and anti-bias efforts can be emotionally heavy, and making connections to learn from and lean on other practitioners can make a significant difference in your personal sustainability and the continued growth of anti-racist efforts within your school or district.
- **Find out what has been done to support these efforts and what has been successful.** Depending on your school size and the level of connectedness

or collaboration between divisions and grades, it can be tricky to keep track of all the work that connects to diversity, equity, and inclusion goals, including schoolwide events and programming, purchased or shared resources, new or adjusted policies and practices, and student involvement. As you think about planning for the future, consider what has already been done, what is currently happening, and what still needs to be done. Then, you can dig deeper to figure out what is working well and how to build on those strengths, reimagine efforts, or abandon those not serving students or families well. Make time to meet with educators to learn about what has occurred within the school. Even if you have been in the school for a few years, you never know what you might learn when you start having intentional conversations about efforts that have been made within the diversity, equity, and inclusion space. I strongly suggest collecting and taking a record of what you learn. Recordkeeping can be an instrumental reference as you and those who come after you push progress forward.

AS YOU THINK ABOUT PLANNING FOR THE FUTURE, CONSIDER WHAT HAS ALREADY BEEN DONE, WHAT IS CURRENTLY HAPPENING, AND WHAT STILL NEEDS TO BE DONE.

A BLUEPRINT FOR FULL IMPLEMENTATION

Step 1: Find strong leadership.

Any large-scale or foundational changes to a school's structures, systems, policies, and practices take the effort and commitment of many. It is critical to appoint an educator to lead efforts as their full-time responsibility to support streamlined and dedicated communication, decision-making, ideation, planning, implementation, and progression of efforts. In many schools or districts, this person is the diversity, equity, and inclusion director or any variation of this title. Be wary of allowing this role to become symbolic or mired in political debates rather than driving change and improvement. Having a leader does not eliminate the need for a committee and schoolwide buy-in (especially in a large school or district). Still, it meets the necessity of consistency, responsiveness, and forward-thinking planning. It is critical to note that this role also requires a dedication of monetary resources. Leading efforts for racial equity is extremely difficult to do as an extra, unpaid, or minimally paid responsibility, and it sends the message that racial equity work or DEI is not valuable. As you seek out someone to step into this leadership role, below are a few questions to consider as you think about what an individual would need to be successful in this position for your school:

- Are they an anti-racist educator who has developed their critical consciousness and sociopolitical lens?
- Do their values align with the school's mission and values?
- Are they willing to do what is best for students and stick to values, even in the face of opposition?
- What qualities do they need to empower others?

Anti-Racist Teaching

- How do they respond to opposition?
- Are they continuing to learn and grow?
- Are they willing to listen to, support, and connect with teachers, students, and families?
- Do they have strong communication skills and a willingness to listen for understanding?

Step 2: Determine areas of need.

Whether the person (or people) leading change has been a longtime member of the school community or is completely new, dedicate time to gathering data to learn about the needs of the school through the perspectives of each constituency. One strategy to do this is through an equity audit. It allows institutions to analyze areas of strength and weakness regarding equity and inclusivity across the school environment, curriculum, instruction, students, families, practices, policies, and other areas. An equity audit can be a massive, multiyear undertaking utilizing various data-collection methodologies. Depending on the resources and "people power" of your school or district, you may also choose to start with a scaled-back version of an equity audit, asking the most pressing questions of the most immediate group that can provide feedback: school staff. Plan to hear from staff, students, and other relevant constituencies, and if time and resources are of the essence, then prioritize where and how to begin. One handy resource is the book *Using Equity Audits to Create Equitable and Excellent Schools* by Linda Skrla, Kathryn McKenzie, and James Joseph Scheurich.

Take the necessary steps to learn about the needs of the community you serve. The results will offer a data-driven approach to determine the most meaningful next steps in creating a more equitable school community. You can collect information through surveys, focus groups, and interviews, as well as by analyzing already-present school data and statistics. While I have condensed my suggestion in this section to a couple of paragraphs, entire books have been written about equity audits. My recommendation is only a starting point to investigate how this essential tool will support your school's aims. Modeled after questions in Hanover Research's brief, "Conducting an Equity Audit," here are five questions to guide you:

- Are our curriculum and instruction equitable and inclusive?
- Are our practices and policies equitable and inclusive?
- Does our school culture reflect and promote values of equity and inclusivity?
- Do staff, students, and family experiences reflect our values of equity and inclusion?
- What are our school's staff, students, and families' perceptions of equity and inclusion?

Step 3: Develop a long-term plan.

Any work you do to create a more inclusive and equitable environment is for the long term, not a one-time activity or single-year focus. It also must continue, even as staff leave and new staff join. Creating a shared living document that outlines or defines a long-term plan is a good tool to communicate and maintain institutional knowledge of what has been done, what's happening, and the plans for the future. It is also a valuable tool to communicate your racial equity work to the stakeholders who want to understand how it fits into the larger vision and mission of the school. Be mindful not to expend more energy creating a document than actually doing work that directly benefits the school community.

You also want to create a document with a long-term plan and refer back to it as you pursue changes.

A wise administrator once told me that, too often, educators work *for* the data rather than making the data work for them. As you collected data throughout these Hacks, and if you chose to conduct an equity audit, make this data work for you. Determine the school's needs based on your collected evidence, and plan realistic, meaningful long-term goals. Depending on the needs and practices of your institution, you may choose to model your goals as SMART goals (Specific, Measurable, Achievable, Relevant, and Time-Bound), a theory of action to keep them short and action-oriented, a mix of these, or any other way that best suits your needs and capacity. However you choose to frame the goals, make them realistic and tied to your school's greater mission and vision. Additionally, goals regarding diversity, equity, or inclusion should not be siloed from other buckets of work within the school or district; weave them into everything and all areas. Here are several questions to guide your goal-setting:

- What is already happening to support our mission and vision, and how can we build on it?
- What are our areas of need, and how can we address them?
- What actions or steps do we need to take to meet these goals?

Step 4: Create avenues for students and staff to share their voices.

Beyond the initial or ongoing data collection, how will you know when to pivot as different needs arise? How will you know when incidents or situations add to the broader context and necessitate new thinking about an action or goal? It's crucial to the relevancy, effectiveness, and meaningfulness of your actions and goals that you ensure there are clear and known pathways for community members to call attention to issues and let their voices be heard. All this is to create a better experience for the school community; therefore, you must constantly consider whether or not community members feel as though they are being heard and their voices are valued. Additionally, even if you set goals that are tied to the mission and vision and address needs based on evidence, you must still maintain flexibility in how the school advances toward those goals so your efforts are relevant and address ongoing needs.

So, what might this avenue look like? It varies depending on the structures and systems already in place at your school. In addition to working directly with the student support team, leaders, teachers, and students, you might also create a way for individuals to reach out for support or to report an issue efficiently and immediately. One example used in many schools is incident reporting forms. These can be set up anonymously or to collect identifying information for follow-up. Use them to ask questions to glean relevant information. Make them broadly available, easily accessible, and self-explanatory. If you choose to implement a useful resource such as this, be intentional about how you share the purpose of it, the location, and what happens once the forms are submitted.

Step 5: Maintain transparency of current efforts and next steps.

Everyone is busy in a school. So busy that sometimes, we get wrapped up in what we are doing and forget about the importance of intentional communication and transparency. When this happens, it can seem like nothing is being done to move progress forward in regard to anti-racist or DEI work. With so many moving pieces in a school and the various ways our endeavors can affect individuals differently, we can take the initiative to be deliberate about sharing plans, goals, and other ongoing actions. Of course, what and how you share with each stakeholder group will be different based on their role in relation to the school, but maintaining transparency and open lines of communication are powerful ways to build trust, garner support, and maintain motivation and momentum.

Communication is especially important for teachers. As a teacher, when I was asked to do something new or differently, my first thought was always, "Why?" Of course, I simply was not privy to such information in my role, but having a better understanding of why and continued communication and transparency about how a process fit into our greater mission and values helped to build understanding and trust. It's critical to create a positive climate and culture where teachers are willing to grow to support the school's mission and vision. As always, the method you use to maintain communication will vary by school. Even if you have a webpage that shares the broader scope of anti-racist efforts, it will likely be more for external community members (i.e., families, board members, and visitors). Here are a few advantages of creating a "living" document to share internally with employees. It can be:

- easily and frequently updated
- accessible anytime
- shared consistently (i.e., monthly, when the committee meets, or any time that meets your school's needs)

OVERCOMING PUSHBACK

You may be faced with challenges and opposition to setting up a plan for long-term change and implementing policies and practices that promote diversity, equity, and inclusion. Although I will share specific responses to possible pushbacks, an unwavering response is that we, educators, are in the business of doing what is best for all students, and this is nonnegotiable.

With teacher burnout and shortages, we can't add more to their plates. It's true that teachers are often already overwhelmed with many mandates and requirements. When a change is not planned well, teachers have not received the proper preparation, and anti-racism has not been established as a school foundation, then yes, a focus on racial equity will feel like an extra thing on their plates. It is essential for teachers to develop a clear understanding of what anti-racism is and is not and to receive ongoing, consistent support. We must explicitly shape our values, practices, and policies for forward progression to occur.

When we take the time to understand how to better support BIPOC students and families, it makes us better at our jobs. The more I learned and grew, the more skills and strategies I had to apply in all situations. I was better prepared to do my work, and my increased capacity made it less stressful and more rewarding. When we are better able to serve the needs of our students, it is a gift that keeps on giving! Having the skills and knowledge to offer stronger support helps us to close the gap between what students need and what we have to offer.

We already have a committee; why do we need a leadership position? It is unsustainable for schools to leave all racial equity efforts to a single individual. Shifting the climate and culture of a school is a schoolwide effort. That being said, having an individual whose sole purpose is to spearhead efforts within the diversity, equity, and inclusion space—along with a committee and the support of the school—is an effective approach when striving to ensure longevity. Benefits of this approach include:

- having a throughline for communication and transparency
- maintaining continuity and consistency in alignment with the mission and vision

- being able to invest in and utilize this individual's knowledge and professional capacity to identify, understand, and formulate solutions to meet the needs of the school community
- ensuring this individual will have the time needed to commit to DEI work
- providing opportunities for high-quality, in-house professional learning as they increase their professional capacity

Community members don't support diversity, equity, and inclusion. Have you heard of the 20/60/20 rule? With any change, 20 percent of people will be completely on board, 60 percent will be a "maybe" and can be influenced, and 20 percent will be in opposition. No matter what, folks will always disagree, and that's okay. Sometimes, those in opposition make their voices the loudest and most disruptive. Thank the supporters and amplify their voices; be transparent and explicit about the purpose and add supporting data and arguments to encourage the "maybes" to offer their support; listen to the opposition but maintain a firm stance about doing what is best for all students. I say to listen because whatever their reasoning may be, if we take time to understand the root of their opposition, we might be able to formulate responses that address their concerns. However, sometimes, nothing can be done to change an individual's stance, and after listening, we must refocus our energy on supporting students and educators. It's also valuable to model "listening" with your students. Be mindful of not allowing the opposition to derail progress.

A recommendation for dealing with difficult oppositional conversations is to learn about and utilize the Courageous Conversation Compass from Glenn Singleton's book *Courageous Conversations About Race*. The four points of the compass are emotional (heart), intellectual (mind), moral (soul), and relational (hands/feet). Use this tool to check the source of your feelings about ideas and topics. When I listen to differing opinions and consider where a person's perspective is coming from, it allows me to have more targeted responses and conversations that are more productive.

THE HACK IN ACTION

In 2023, I began working as the director of diversity, equity, inclusion, and belonging (DEIB) for an independent Catholic school. After the departure of the previous coordinator in this role, the school began a year-long search for a full-time director. As a small school serving almost two hundred students in kindergarten through twelfth grade, they were searching for someone whose values aligned with their forward-thinking vision. This individual would need to take time to understand the unique needs of the school community and be highly motivated yet discerning to move progress forward at a pace that would result in success. While the school was largely white and located in a suburb near a large city, it served students from over forty zip codes. The population's religious and racial diversity was also growing.

In my first phone call to connect with the head of the school, the importance of the school's mission, vision, and values was made clear, as well as honesty about where they were and where they would like to be regarding diversity, equity, and inclusion. What stood out to me was the alignment of our values. We wanted to do what was best for students and understood that creating inclusive and affirming spaces was critical to this intention. It was paramount to listen to those in the school who shared historically marginalized identities.

When I started in the position, my priority was to learn about the school. Some areas I wanted to learn more about were:

- school history, mission, vision, and goals
- staff experiences with anti-racism and other topics related to diversity, equity, inclusion, and belonging
- school efforts, initiatives, and professional learning of the past
- student and staff demographics
- staff, student, and family perceptions of the climate and culture

I wanted to learn as much as I could to inform the next steps for the future. Building trusting relationships with colleagues, students, and families was also essential. Trust is vital to moving progress forward, and as a newcomer to a small community, I understood the great significance of taking the time to get to know the community and make connections. By learning about the school and connecting with people, I would also learn more about the school's traditions, values, and identity.

Since it was summertime when I joined and most of the community was off campus enjoying summer vacation, I started by learning as much as possible about the local and school history and the mission, vision, and goals. I had a lot of information to digest, but one imperative in my learning was to develop an understanding of the school's values on paper and in practice. In other words, what do we say we believe and value, and how do our actions align? I used that time to learn about the goals involving my role as the director of DEIB and investigated how much had been accomplished. My learning gave me a good starting point to decipher what I would need to learn more about once the school year began, where time and efforts had been invested, and what progress we had made.

For example, one goal was to continue providing education in the diversity, equity, inclusion, and belonging space. While this

Plan for Longevity

means that students continue being directly involved in DEIB work, staff must continue developing their professional capacity to engage students effectively and affirmatively. As a result, my next goal when the school year began, in addition to getting to know everyone, was to learn about their professional learning experiences within diversity, equity, inclusion, and belonging. I wanted to get a sense of what folks felt challenged by. As a former teacher, I knew what it was like to struggle and not feel I had the tools to improve, regardless of my motivation. So, I created and shared a survey to understand my colleagues' previous professional learning and what they still wanted to learn about. Later, I would use this information to inform my planning for professional learning and other support and guidance offered to teachers.

As the school year progressed, I took opportunities to talk with staff members and hear more about their personal stories and perceptions of DEIB efforts within our school. This "listening" work was essential to add context to what I had learned in the professional learning survey. It also helped me to understand the needs and strengths of students and staff more profoundly. These conversations revealed organizational history and shared feelings that influenced how we move forward for the most positive outcomes. The more I learned, the more questions I had, and the more I sought guidance.

Thankfully, as I settled into my position, I was connected to a vast network of fellow directors of diversity, equity, and inclusion and other DEI practitioners who were familiar with the structure of independent schools and helpful in offering strategies to learn more. Coming from a public school setting, I realized I had much to learn about independent schools. One DEI consultant with a long history of attending and working in independent schools suggested that I conduct a scaled-back equity audit to dig deeper into the school's specific needs. As with any school, there are so many potential areas to make a priority, but it was essential to spend time in my first year figuring out what would be the most meaningful and impactful. I also collected data that was key to understanding the needs of our community, who was in our community, and what perspectives they brought with them.

After much research about what this scaled-back equity audit could look like, I created a survey with the help of a colleague that would offer more insight about our strengths and opportunities for growth within the realms of the school environment, curriculum and instruction, students, community and parents, school practice and culture, and school policy. The data provided me with valuable information that confirmed the positive results of initiatives already happening, reiterated areas we knew we needed to improve, and highlighted priorities that needed to be at the forefront or re-evaluated. With this data and everything else I learned, I could look at our goals through a more informed perspective, determine the most pressing needs, and establish the steps to accomplish them. Furthermore, I started thinking about how to capture family and student voices later in the school year.

While collecting data to undergird our efforts, I also revived and created crucial facets of the school's former and future DEIB actions. The first was a bias incident reporting form that had been shared with the school community. The form provided all members of the school community with an avenue to be heard and receive support when an incident caused harm to an individual due to bias. Not only did this help amplify students' voices, but it also provided a method of documentation, a record of accountability, and an expectation of repairing the harm.

I also restored the school's faculty diversity, equity, inclusion, and belonging committee. As part of my learning, I gained some understanding of what the committee had done in the past and the structure of their work. Committee members had made progress around student programming, community building, and

Plan for Longevity

professional learning. However, without a DEIB director, the continuity of the group faded. In addition to continuing endeavors they had already started, this group was instrumental in providing feedback and input for larger DEIB goals and changes the department could support or make. One small yet significant idea during the first meeting was the importance of transparency. Teachers new to the school had questions about topics I took for granted as common knowledge, which prompted me to create a DEIB newsletter for the internal community. The newsletter would be a "living" document to house DEIB resources, updates, and announcements. Coming from my classroom role in an elementary school to directing a department that provided guidance to a K–12 school, I needed to be more intentional in my communication about what was happening across the lower, middle, and upper school divisions since so many different pockets of work were present.

We had plenty of moments of challenge and growth. The most evident challenge at this time was simply being new and unaware. Knowing the importance of talking with teachers and community members to get a deeper, authentic understanding of the school, yet having to wait to start those conversations, required me to be even more conscious and cautious of my assumptions and perceptions, especially since I was coming from a public-school environment that served a different population. I needed to check my own biases. I also had to be honest about what I didn't know and be willing to ask many questions. Another challenge was being a department of one. As a teacher, I was used to having a circle of fellow teachers to collaborate with on my team or in the building. As a DEIB director, I could consult with others, get feedback, bounce ideas, and lean on their DEIB knowledge, but I would still be the only person in my role. Thankfully, the head of the school was great about connecting me to other DEI directors, and I could join online events that were explicitly for DEI leaders in independent schools. These opportunities offered me a wealth of advice and ideas from individuals in the same position I was in.

The knowledge, data, and insights all informed the creation of a long-term plan to see growth and impact in our school's diversity, equity, inclusion, and belonging efforts. From the moment I began this role, I wanted to be intentional about planning for longevity so that no matter who is in this position, we know what has been done, what we are doing, and what we need to do in the future, allowing our efforts to continue seamlessly. By learning about the specific needs of our school and using this information to shape goals that uplift the mission and vision, we can move forward in ways that are meaningful and necessary to the long-term growth of the school—growth that would require a foundational value of anti-racism and an environment that is inclusive and affirming.

Taking the time to learn about a school community and analyze the needs that may not be evident is imperative to making long-term goals and plans that will effect change. With the tumultuous landscape of education, open communication pathways and increased transparency help to develop trust and understanding of what students and staff need and are experiencing. Let's commit to creating an environment where *every* student feels seen, heard, and valued, and let's take action to figure out why that's not happening yet and strive to get there.

CONCLUSION
KEEP MOVING FORWARD

Treating different things the same can generate as much inequality as treating the same things differently.
— KIMBERLÉ CRENSHAW, SCHOLAR AND WRITER

WHEN WE ARE committed to using our roles and influence in ways that give power to truth, it amplifies the voices of those who have been, and continue to be, oppressed and disempowered. However, we must also be cognizant of our emotional well-being. As you aim to make your school more equitable and inclusive, you will find the highs and lows along the journey. Some days, you will feel motivated and empowered. On others, you might feel disillusioned and discouraged. Nevertheless, every day that we go to school and support students, families, and colleagues, we do the type of work that is much bigger than ourselves. Because of the weight of racial equity efforts, it is imperative to care for your emotional capacity and seek out supportive communities that also champion values of diversity, equity, and inclusion. As we pour out ourselves, uncovering our implicit biases and braving potentially uncomfortable conversations, we can replenish ourselves by intentionally finding joy and celebrating moments of success and growth.

Whether it's the culture to which we contribute, our work to change policies that once upheld white supremacy, or our interactions that let every student know they are worthy and highly valued, we owe it to our students, and even to ourselves, to do what we can to create an environment where students and staff feel a sense of joy and affirmation as they move throughout their days. By making the intentional moves discussed throughout this book, you can:

- Support educators in their growth as anti-racist practitioners who understand the complexities and importance of identity so they can support students in ways that are empowering and responsive to oppressive systems and structures.

- Adopt a proactive approach to recruiting and retaining BIPOC educators by providing opportunities and spaces that recognize and respond to their needs and lived experiences.

- Cultivate inclusive classrooms that invite all students to show up as their whole, authentic selves and offer a rich learning environment.

- Learn about the families you serve and create meaningful ways for them to engage.

- Create a sustainable leadership structure and a plan for the long-term growth and impact of anti-racist work.

While you learn and plan for what you can do within your school, you will uncover challenges and pushback. In the face of resistance to anti-racism, hold firm to core values and do what is right for students while also giving yourself and others grace. Sometimes, we will make mistakes or situations will go differently than planned. The key is to learn lessons from these mistakes, keep growing, continue putting in the effort, and avoid discouragement. From benefiting a single student to shifting the entire culture and climate of a school, anti-racism has the power to make a difference and provide the educational experience all students deserve.

ABOUT THE AUTHOR

Symone James Abiola is an educator who has served students and families as a teacher and diversity, equity, and inclusion practitioner. In 2022, Symone was honored with the Excellence in Equity: Champion of Equity–General Education Teacher Award, presented by The American Consortium for Equity in Education. Her work has been motivated by the belief that every student deserves to leave their kindergarten through twelfth-grade educational experience with the skills to think critically about the world, a strong sense of self, and confidence in who they are and what they can accomplish. She is also passionate about supporting fellow educators in gaining the knowledge and resources they need to create welcoming, equitable school environments where all students can thrive and feel they belong.

Symone holds a Sixth-Year Diploma in Educational Administration, a Master of Arts degree in Curriculum and Instruction, and a Bachelor of Science degree in Elementary Education with a minor in Diversity Studies in American Culture, all from the University of Connecticut.

Connect with Symone and access more resources through her website, symonejamesabiola.com.

ACKNOWLEDGMENTS

FIRST, I HAVE to thank God for this opportunity to share what I have learned with others and for guiding me in the uncharted territory of writing a book. I thank my husband, Oljaide, who supported me through every step of this process—whether that meant putting off plans so I could write, bringing me a cup of tea and dinner late at night, or sharing words of encouragement—I am so grateful for you.

Thank you to my parents, Seymour and Michelle, and my sister, Brittney, for all of their encouragement and support and for always sharing words of empowerment and nurturance as I chugged along in the writing process. Because of you, Ma and Dad, I have never questioned my self-worth in the face of adversity.

Thank you to my family and in-law family, and specifically my mother-in-law, Toni—I truly appreciate every prayer you said as I pushed to finish this book.

A huge shout out and deepest gratitude to all the folks who shared their time with me so I could interview them—Lysette, Orlando, Jason, Tracey, and Natalie—I appreciate y'all more than words can express! Lysette, I owe you special thanks for submitting me for the award in the first place and for all the words of encouragement; if not for you, this wouldn't have happened!

Thank you to my friends who checked in and offered words of support—you are appreciated! Especially Tracey, you are a real one, and I am grateful for your friendship, feedback, and support always.

Shout out to my former colleagues in Meriden who cheered me on and supported the work discussed in this book. Thank you so much to the Times 10 Publishing Team. I am so grateful for the opportunity to share what I have learned with the education community in a way that feels true to my voice. It has been a transformative experience, and you have my deepest appreciation. And finally, a special note of gratitude to the many brilliant educators whom I have learned from over the years.

SNEAK PEEK

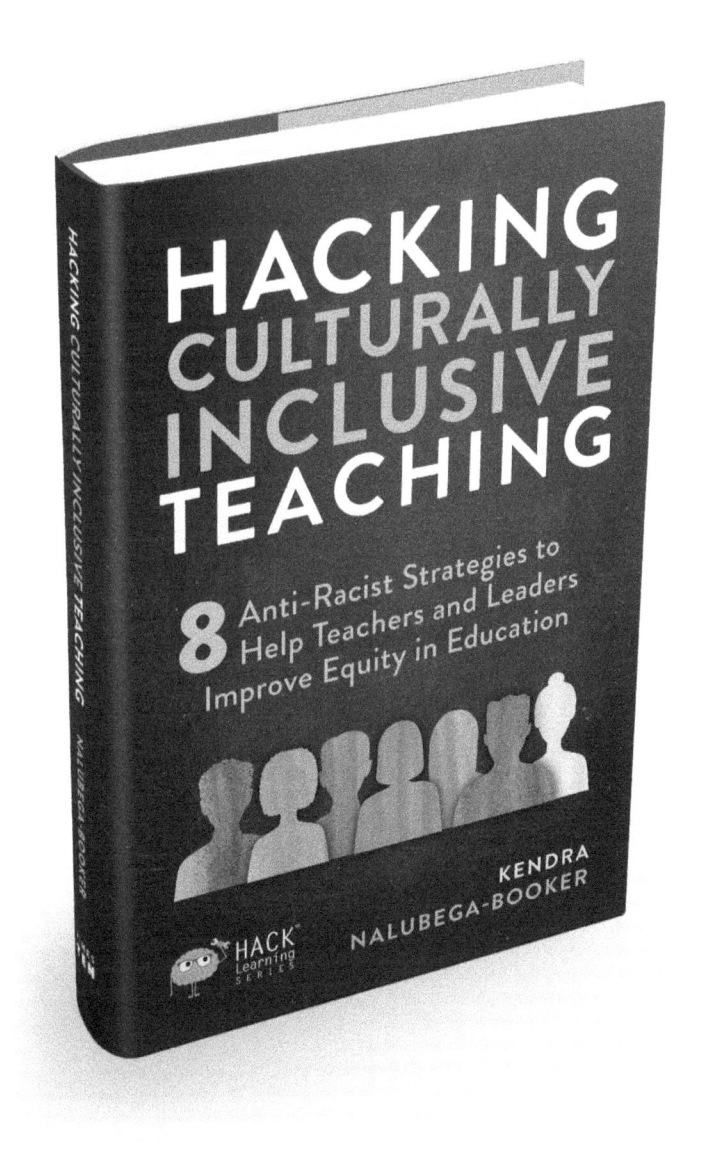

HACK 3

EMPLOY TRANSLANGUAGING METHODS

Use Students' Home Languages and Cultures as a Resource

Before students can use their language as a critical resource to build new skills, they must be able to view their language as intellectually valuable.
— APRIL BAKER-BELL, TRANSDISCIPLINARY TEACHER AND ACTIVIST

THE PROBLEM: EDUCATION PROGRAMS DO NOT EQUIP TEACHERS WITH THE NECESSARY TOOLS

IT IS OUR responsibility as educators to meet our students where they are and provide them with the necessary tools for success without lowering our expectations.

Racialized students in the US experience overlapping forms of academic, linguistic, and racial prejudice. According to the National Center for Education Statistics, in the 2017–18 school year, 79 percent of public school teachers were White and non-Hispanic, which explains the lack of representation of racialized teachers in classrooms. As a result, thousands of Black, Latinx, and Indigenous students attend schools where there are no same-race teachers or where they are taught by teachers from different ethnic backgrounds. Most teachers likely have limited knowledge about their students' histories and cultures.

Naturally, we know more about our own communities. The lack of multicultural representation in schools or the curriculum has been studied for decades, but the gap between theory and practice persists.

Pierre Bourdieu extended a theory of linguistic exchange that said, in effect, "The properties of the market (jobs, institutions, assessment tools, technologies) determine the value of the linguistic products. Some 'products' hold a higher value than others." This is a prime example of the colonial, racist logic that fuels raciolinguistic ideologies, even in education. When we do not value students' diverse languages, it clearly shows, and they can internalize that. Evidently, we, as educators, must work on bridging the gap between literature and practice, creating opportunities for better academic experiences and ending unnecessary academic setbacks for both teachers and students.

Traditional instruction is aimed toward mainstream students, and teachers sometimes lack the skills required to provide language-minority students access to the English curriculum. This also opens up additional opportunities for students who are monolingual and speak standard English, while linguistically diverse students take on unfair responsibilities to "assimilate" or "blend in." Research shows us that monolingual, English-speaking instructors often enable White, English-dominant students to disrupt, extend, and dominate learning processes. In contrast, bilingual, two-way immersion teachers more often strive to balance students' positions and authority, which nurtures linguistic diversity.

Nelson Flores and Ofelia García published "A Critical Review of Bilingual Education in the United States," and in it, they remind us of two goals of bilingual education that emerged in the post–civil rights era: 1) for the programs to improve the self-esteem of linguistically and culturally diverse students (LCDS) by instilling confidence, and 2) for the programs to address the multilingualism of LCDS by giving them a solid foundation in their first language.

Transitional bilingual education (TBE) makes up most bilingual education programs in the United States. Although TBE programs can serve non-English language groups, most serve Spanish-speaking students. This remains a challenge because student demographics are rapidly changing, and schools can't account for many languages. The extent of diverse language representation in US bilingual education varies by state and district.

Generally, the most commonly taught language in bilingual education is Spanish. According to the US Department of Education, in the 2016–17 school year, most bilingual programs utilized Spanish (83 percent), followed by French (7 percent), Chinese (3 percent), Vietnamese (2 percent), and Arabic (1 percent).

However, African/Black languages are barely offered, even though Black immigrants continue to increase in schools. This is a challenge for students needing linguistic resources and teaching strategies that will nurture their home and school languages. Research frequently records contradictions between policy and reality. Although bilingual programs promise students and parents that they will nurture their home languages, many teachers employ "assimilative" practices, prioritizing standard English over other languages to maintain monolingual ideologies.

Another challenge lies in using programs built through categorization, although we have varying capabilities among students. For example, Dual Language Education is another form of Bilingual Education, divided into three types of dual language programs: immersion programs, two-way immersion programs, and developmental or dual language programs in languages other than English. The goal is to develop bilingualism.

> *Translanguaging is a process in which a student draws on multiple languages to express themselves or to enhance their communication.*

It can be challenging for most racialized students with underrepresented languages to thrive in bilingual programs. Multilingual learners benefit more when encouraged to use their knowledge in one language to enhance their proficiency in another language, which calls for educators to embrace and capitalize on students' linguistic diversity and cultural and experiential knowledge.

Overall standard curricula and schools often underappreciate or don't acknowledge the depth of cultural knowledge and values that culturally diverse students possess. Researchers urge teachers to engage with the life experiences of multicultural students in academic and social settings by appreciating the rich cultural diversity these students bring to the classroom and gaining an understanding of it.

THE HACK: EMPLOY TRANSLANGUAGING METHODS

Scholars emphasize the significance of understanding culturally and linguistically diverse student populations. It is critical that educators acknowledge the value that students' languages bring and be intentional about how we influence student perceptions regarding their linguistics. When we tap into *translanguaging*, a process in which a student draws on multiple languages to express themselves or to enhance their communication, we can ensure that each multilingual student uses and honors their full linguistic repertoire.

What does translanguaging look like in the classroom? Teachers use a holistic approach, taking into account all students' linguistic and cognitive abilities to make meaning or comprehend the classroom material being taught in a language different from theirs. Integrating anti-racist, asset-based, and critical language pedagogy (such as translanguaging) would put teachers in a better position to disrupt current practices that perpetuate linguistic injustices.

Translanguaging can provide students with access to classroom content, enhance participation and engagement with the curriculum, help build strong relationships between students and their teachers, and support students in representing their linguistic diversity. It also challenges the "two solitudes" method of bilingualism, suggesting that multilingual speakers transfer between languages instead of using their full linguistic repertoires such as registers, styles, dialects, and accents.

Others point out the political and disruptive nature of translanguaging, revealing how it enables linguistically minoritized students to have opportunities to critique and push against monoglossic ideologies. Teachers must shift toward a translingual approach that views linguistic diversity as a resource for meaning-making in writing, speaking, reading, and listening rather than a deficit or hindrance. The Bell Foundation contends that encouraging bilingual, multilingual, and culturally diverse students to use their entire linguistic repertoire empowers them and helps them utilize their full learning potential.

Teachers can develop a supportive attitude toward multilingualism, which numerous experts and activists continuously advocate as the ideal. Tove Skutnabb-Kangas and others criticized what they viewed as linguicism and created the term "linguistic human rights." According to Shawn Levy et al., when schools view a student's first language negatively, those students may feel less included. Jean Conteh states that valuing multilingualism and linguistic diversity in classrooms helps racialized students succeed. Students can show up as their whole selves, integrate their home languages and cultures, and experience an improved learning experience when teachers value their languages. In research published by Ofelia García, Susana Ibarra Johnson, and Kate Seltzer, they outlined four objectives for the thoughtful inclusion of translanguaging in the classroom:

1. Allowing students to practice their language skills in academic settings

2. Allowing multilingual students and different modes of knowing

3. Fostering students' socioemotional development and bilingual identities

4. Assisting students in understanding difficult texts and subject matter

Planning and gathering the necessary resources can achieve these goals in your classroom. When teachers implement translanguaging strategies, they enable students to feel comfortable and engaged in otherwise difficult and isolating learning environments. It also allows students to share their language and subject-matter knowledge with their classmates. Teachers who provide multilingual learning opportunities for their students cultivate a classroom environment where each student works not only within their developmental level—but also within their comfort zone.

This fosters cross-cultural communication in the classroom and enhances student participation and self-esteem. Ask yourself questions regarding the four goals that García, Johnson, and Seltzer proposed, such as:

1. How am I already providing opportunities for students to develop linguistic skills in academic contexts?

2. Have I created space for my multilingual students and their diverse ways of knowing?

3. How do I support my bilingual and multilingual students' identities and their socioemotional development?

4. How do I plan on supporting my students as they engage with and comprehend complex materials?

As you reflect on your responses, consider the core components of teachers' translanguaging pedagogy in Image 3.1.

COMPONENT	APPLICATION	EXAMPLES
 STANCE	Adopt the belief that it's essential to tap into your students' varied linguistic practices.	Not prioritizing one language over the other(s).
 DESIGN	Use students' language practices to guide instructional design, units, lesson plans, and assessments.	Do this when introducing new concepts and incorporating different spellings and pronunciations.
 SHIFT	Be flexible and openly alter your instructional plan based on student input, performance, and understanding.	Not translating everything encourages students to use their home languages in the same language or cultural small groups.

Image 3.1: Core components of translanguaging pedagogy.

For Black students specifically, I propose the Afrolinguistic capital framework—which situates African and African descendants' linguistic practices as valuable, necessary, and sufficient. Bourdieu's concept of capital suggests that there are different forms of capital, not just economic capital in the real sense but also cultural capital, such as knowledge, skills, other cultural acquisitions, symbolic capital, and more. Regarding linguistic capital, Bourdieu states that different speakers possess different quantities of it. Specifically, it refers to the capacity in which they can manipulate expressions for a "market" (such as an institution or job). Bourdieu's theory of practice and overall work on language and power tended to favor dominant European languages such as French and English. His conceptualization of linguistic capital and the linguistic marketplace contributed to exclusive racist rhetoric that devalues racialized languages even here in the US to this day. Hence the need for the raciolinguistic perspective and application of frameworks such as Afrolinguistic capital to counter these harmful ideologies. In this case, the framework would aid educators in applying translanguaging methods for Black students. Cultural capital is not only limited to an individual but should extend to families and larger groups of people. Teachers should adopt the same attitudes toward Black students to disrupt language-based discrimination and the stigmatization of their diverse linguistic expression.

WHAT YOU CAN DO TOMORROW

The purpose of implementing translanguaging methods is to stimulate and facilitate the use of a student's holistic linguistic repertoire. As students become more acclimated to translanguaging, it becomes more natural for both students and teachers. Educators can apply the same strategies to "mainstream" classes. Here are ideas you can put into practice right away.

BUY
HACKING CULTURALLY INCLUSIVE TEACHING

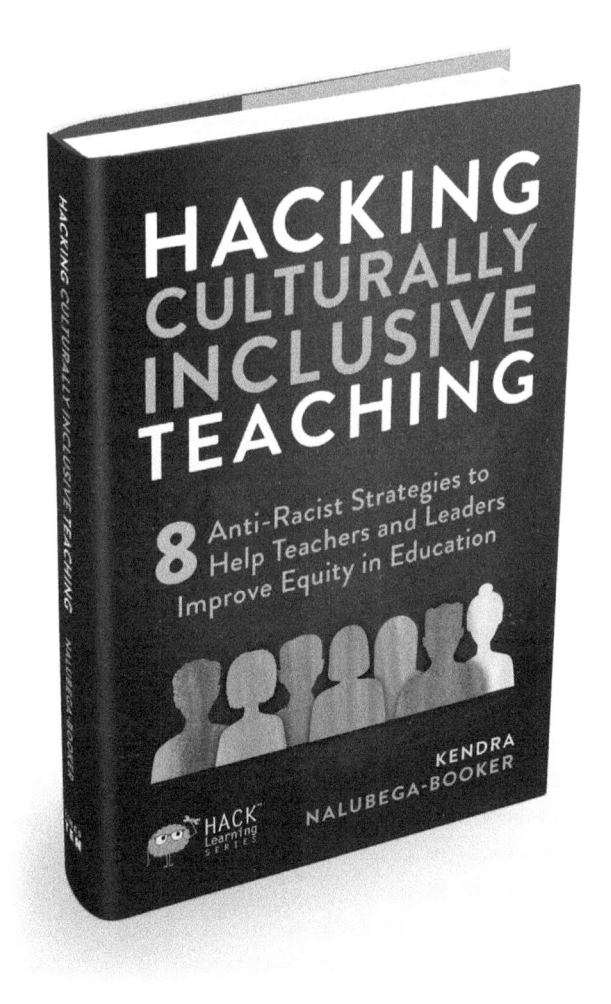

AVAILABLE AT:
Amazon.com
10Publications.com
and bookstores near you

MORE FROM
TIMES 10 PUBLICATIONS

Hacking School Discipline
9 Ways to Create a Culture of Empathy & Responsibility Using Restorative Justice
By Nathan Maynard and Brad Weinstein

Reviewers proclaim this Washington Post Bestseller as "maybe the most important book a teacher can read, a must for all educators, fabulous, a game changer!" Learn how to eliminate punishment and build a culture of responsible students and independent learners. Twenty-one straight months at #1 on Amazon, *Hacking School Discipline* is disrupting education like nothing we've seen in decades—maybe centuries.

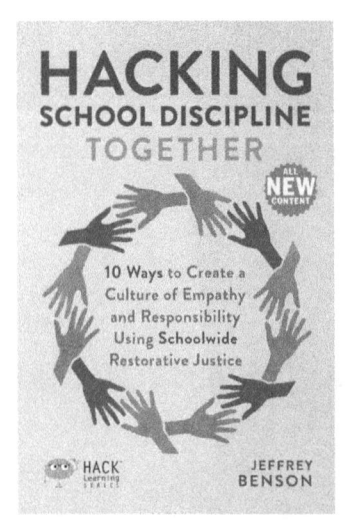

Hacking School Discipline TOGETHER
10 Ways to Create a Culture of Empathy and Responsibility Using Schoolwide Restorative Justice
By Jeffrey Benson

This sequel to *Hacking School Discipline* is for teachers, administrators, and staff who long to create a school that fosters responsibility, forgiveness, and accountability so students learn from their impulsive decisions. We can change the status quo in which students believe their biggest mistake was getting caught. Instead, learn how to create a school where administrators and staff trust each other, and students benefit from what we do best: educate.

Hacking Deficit Thinking
8 Reframes That Will Change the Way You Think about Strength-Based Practices and Equity in Schools
By Byron McClure and Kelsie Reed

Too many teachers focus on what's wrong with their students instead of what's strong. A focus on weakness is a pervasive, powerful judgment that harms students long after they leave school. It's time for educators to reframe teaching and learning. McClure and Reed show how to unlearn student blame and reframe thinking to focus on students' strengths, benefiting them for life.

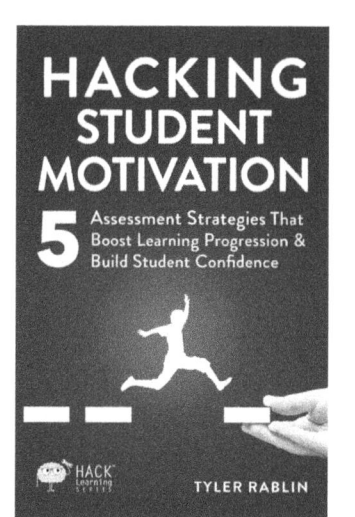

Hacking Student Motivation
5 Assessment Strategies That Boost Learning Progression & Build Student Confidence
By Tyler Rablin

No educator wants to see students defeated when they fail an assessment. Instead, teachers can develop new assessment structures that tap into what we know about motivation and the brain. Rablin shows educators how to efficiently create powerful and motivating assessment practices where failure is a part of learning, assessment is an ongoing process, and growth is the focus for everyone in the room.

AI Goes to School
How to Harness Artificial Intelligence in Education to Prepare Students for the Future (and Make You an Even Better Teacher)
By Micah Miner

Now, educators can prepare themselves and their students for an AI-abundant future by applying AI tools in teaching and communicating. You'll feel empowered, not overpowered, when you explore generative AI tools that produce text and images, delve into AI art, and address the controversies of their use in K–12 education. Transform AI tools into assets for meaningful human connections and effective student learning.

Preventing Polarization
50 Strategies for Teaching Kids about Empathy, Politics, and Civic Responsibility
By Michelle Blanchet and Brian Deters

In an era that has become incredibly polarized politically and socially, we can help our students learn to come together despite differences and become active and engaged citizens. A one-off civics course is not enough. Learn essential strategies to create experiences that help students break down barriers through activities and role-playing. Let's show our students how to make a difference, minimize conflict, and build accord.

TIMES 10 PUBLICATIONS provides practical solutions that busy people can read today and use tomorrow. We bring you content from experienced researchers and practitioners, and we share it through books, podcasts, webinars, articles, events, and ongoing conversations on social media. Our books and materials help turn practice into action. Stay in touch with us at 10Publications.com and follow our updates @10Publications.